Clicheionary
HOW TO PLAY WITH WORDS

Patrick Murphy

PublishAmerica
Baltimore

© 2005 by Patrick Murphy.
All rights reserved. No part of this book may be reproduced, stored in a retrieval system or transmitted in any form or by any means without the prior written permission of the publishers, except by a reviewer who may quote brief passages in a review to be printed in a newspaper, magazine or journal.

First printing

ISBN: 1-4137-6391-X
PUBLISHED BY PUBLISHAMERICA, LLLP
www.publishamerica.com
Baltimore

Printed in the United States of America

This book is dedicated to everyone who made it possible. I compiled the expressions after hearing them spoken by many different people in many different places over a long period of time. I thank each and every one of you from the bottom of my heart. Also, I owe a debt of gratitude to LongRidge WritersGroup for spurring me on to write by putting me doggedly to the task.

Take it with a grain of salt: doubt it, question it, and above all, don't take it too seriously.

Clicheionary
HOW TO PLAY WITH WORDS

A bird in the hand is worth two in the bush: make safe investments. Don't go chasing after rainbows.

A blade of grass is a blade of grass: nature is repetitious

A bundle of nerves: all tied up in knots

A cushion: money set aside for an emergency

A delicate balance: dividing your time between work, family, recreation, and rest

A dinosaur: extinct, obsolete, or soon to be

A dog's life: the finer aspects of living. All of the virtues, none of the vices. "Virtue unable to make itself man, became beast" (Victor Hugo).

A drop in the bucket: an insignificant amount

A fancy Dan: an innovative dresser

A few bad apples don't spoil the whole bunch: you can't judge the whole by the sum of its parts

A foregone conclusion: inevitable

A Godsend: there when you needed it most

A green thumb: master of horticulture

A hard life: no faith

A house divided cannot stand: unsettled disputes spell certain failure

A kick in the ass: to keep you going

A leopard never changes its spots: a fool is a fool is a fool

A lifesaver: Jesus Christ. "I am the Way, the Truth, and the Life" (New Testament).

A light touch: delicately applied

A little bit of this and a little bit of that: moderation

A little breathing room: time to catch up

A little piece of heaven: peace and quiet in your own little corner of the world

A loose cannon: someone who loses their temper with little or no provocation

A loose tongue: not keeping a secret, letting the cat out of the bag

A necessary evil: the justice system. Crime does pay for those who administer it.

A parting thought: fare thee well. "To have endless leisure, in the sun and in the snow, without pain, without pleasure" (Edward Thomas).

A pat on the back: offering encouragement

A pat on the head: congratulations, good work

A picture is worth a thousand words: seeing is believing

A piece of the action: divide the net profit of a joint enterprise among the participants according to their input

A place in the sun: owning an adequate amount of land

A place to hang your hat: some space of your own

A real bummer: a mildly depressing event in your life

A real gun: excelling at throwing

A real handful: difficult to control

A real live one: a gambler. "His face was a book where men might read strange matters" (William Shakespeare).

A real operator: a true entrepreneur and a major player in the field of economics

A red flag: a call for vigilance. Highlighted.

A ring around your finger: married or betrothed

A rock: a poker player who only plays the very best starting hands. You can read them like a book.

A rolling stone gathers no moss: stay active no matter what your situation is and you won't become rusty

A roof over your head: shelter

A round in the chamber: ready to be used if needed

A rude awakening: something happened that made you realize you aren't as smart as you think you are

A rush: on a lucky streak

A second chance: starting over again with a clean slate, like being born again

A setup: a trap prepared in advance to snare someone

A shady background: your past may incriminate you. Take the Fifth.

A short fuse: ready to explode emotionally. Temper, temper.

A shoot-out: a high-scoring sporting event

A shot in the arm: a quick picker-upper

A shot in the dark: high odds against it

A shoulder to cry on: always there for you

A silver tongue: the gift of gab, well-spoken

A sleeper: merit soon to emerge. "Slowly rises worth, out of poverty depressed" (Samuel Johnson).

A smoking gun: be wary of it, cause for concern

As much as you can: live and love

A soft touch: easy to borrow from. "Neither a borrower nor a lender be" (William Shakespeare).

A square: a total bore

A squeaker: just made it

A step in the right direction: discarding bad habits and beginning to live the good life

A stepping stone: the Earth. "If you're going through hell, keep going" (Winston Churchill).

A straight answer: as close to the truth as you can come

A tall order: difficult to fulfill

A taste of your own medicine: you got what you deserve

A thorn in your side: it must be removed to prevent it from impeding your progress

A tightwad: miserly, cheap

A two-way street: what comes around goes around. Do someone wrong and somewhere along the line it will come right back at you.

A vicious cycle: life and death

A way of life: irresistible attractions

A way with women: treating them nice

A weak spot: everyone has one. What's yours?

A wild fling: a brief love affair

A word to the wise is sufficient: an explanation from a friend is enough to convince you that you were incorrect

Above and beyond the call of duty: giving 110%

Accidents happen: nevertheless, the majority of them can be attributed to negligence

According to their just desserts: "The world passes but whoever does the Word of the Lord lives forever" (Bible).

A/C, D/C: bisexual

Act like a man: stand on your own two feet. "He who lets loose the beast in himself, puts away the pain of being a man" (Samuel Johnson).

Act your age: an adult behaving like a child. Grow up.

Actions speak louder than words: conserve your energy by making every one of your actions count for something. "Words full of deceit, boasts, insults, and threats soil you from within" (New Testament).

Add another feather to your cap: one more noteworthy achievement

Add insult to injury: making matters worse

Add spice to it: when playing the role, add a little of this but try not to overdo it

Adult entertainment: a euphemism for smut. Profitable debauchery.

Afraid of your own shadow: a coward. "Cowards die a thousand times, the valiant but once" (William Shakespeare).

After all is said and done: there's nothing you can do about it

Against my better judgment: I'm going to do it anyway

Ahead of your time: acting and thinking like people will in many years to come

Ain't that a bitch: so sorry for you

All bent out of shape: not your usual self. Fit to be tied.

All bets are off: your part of the bargain wasn't kept, so I don't have to keep mine

All choked up: emotional

All ears: listening carefully. "Give your ears to all, your tongue to few" (William Shakespeare).

All good things must end: say goodbye with class and no remorse. "Though inland far we be, our souls have sight of that immortal sea" (William Wordsworth).

All hell broke loose: extreme chaos

All hopped up: high as a kite

All hype and psyche: advertising

All in a day's work: breathing, drinking, eating, thinking, motion, manipulation, and then "Sleep that knits the raveled sleeve of care, sore labor's bath, balm for hurt minds, the death of each day's life, chief nourisher in life's feast" (William Shakespeare).

All is vanity: everyone has a high opinion of themselves and seek to gain all they can. In all events, "Golden lads and girls all must like chimney sweepers come to dust" (Unknown).

All over the map: erratic

All people are created equal: to pay bills, to collect bills, to chase money. "I can't go on, I will go on" (Samuel Beckett).

All played out: tired of the night life

All right, already: I'll do it, but reluctantly

All roads lead to Rome: the center of economical activity. The seat of power.

All shapes and forms: everything under the sun

All that for nothing: futility

All that glitters is not gold: some things that appear to be valuable are not

All the comforts of home: necessities, some luxuries, love, pets, family. "Lord, remember me and mine, with mercy's temporal and divine" (Robert Burns).

All the ins and outs: the inside scoop

All things being equal: life is equally dear to all living things. "He prays best who loves best all things great and small" (Samuel Coleridge).

All thumbs: not agile, clumsy, awkward

All washed up: a has-been, through

All work and no play: not if you mix business and pleasure

All your troubles will soon be over: who knows where or when. "There are two tragedies in life, getting what you want and not getting what you want" (Oscar Wilde).

All's well that ends well: death by natural causes. "Whatever fades but fading pleasure brings" (Unknown).

Along for the ride: accompaniment

Always looking at the world through rose-colored glasses: invariably seeing only the bright side of life

Amazing powers of concentration: maximizing your senses

An accident waiting to happen: extremely careless, tantamount to a fool. "Don't suffer fools gladly" (William Shakespeare).

An ace in the hole: a resource held back in case of need

An art form in itself: doing anything exceptionally well

An educated guess: if you're educated

An eager beaver: a zealous volunteer

An eyebrow raiser: the validity of the outcome is highly questionable

An eye for an eye, a tooth for a tooth: make the punishment fit the crime

An eye opener: an alcoholic drink upon awakening

An Iron Curtain: totalitarianism in control of a country

An off-the-cuff remark: blurting out something, unrehearsed

An ounce of prevention is worth a pound of cure: maintenance can prevent a breakdown in the future. "Oh build your ship of death. Oh build it! For you will need it. For the voyage of oblivion awaits you" (David Lawrence).

And I don't mean maybe: what you just said is unequivocal

And the beat goes on: children inherit what's left to them

Another day, another dollar: you need money to survive. Money can't buy happiness but it sure comes close.

Another dimension: try to reach it, if you dare

Another nail in your coffin: taking a breath of polluted air

Apple of your eye: someone you love very much

Are you asking me or telling me?: where are you coming from?

Are you blind?: you should have seen it

Armed and dangerous: a macho misunderstanding

Armed to the teeth: an inferiority complex

Around and around we go: the cycle of existence

As good as gold: verifiable. You can take it to the bank.

As plain as the nose on your face: you should have noticed it. "Out of the mouth of babes and sucklings praise is perfect" (New Testament).

As sure as I'm sitting here: I'm certain that it's true

As the crow flies: in a straight line. From point A to point B.

As we all know too well: "Things on Earth seem permanent but they are less permanent than a shadow" (William Blake).

At a crossroads: forced to decide which way to go

At the bottom of a bottomless pit: impossible to find

At the dawn of a new era: great changes will occur. "And intellect its wandering to this, and that, and the other thing, deliver us from the crime of death and birth" (William Butler Yeats).

At the drop of a hat: immediately

At the end of your rope: nothing left, finished

At the spur of the moment: doing it without much thought beforehand

At the top of your game: the best that you can do

At this point in time: right now, presently

At this stage of the game: it's time to call it quits

At your beckon call: a servant. Most rich people use and abuse them.

At your wit's end: a very difficult problem indeed

B

Back from the dead: said to or about someone who was very ill but recovered

Back in the good old days: when life was mellow, oh so mellow

Back in the saddle: you're in control again

Back to square one: starting over again completely

Back to the drawing board: it was incorrect, so try it again a different way

Back to the salt mines: going to work to earn your daily keep. "Have I not reason to lament, what man has made of man" (William Wordsworth).

Bad publicity: there's no such thing in the entertainment business

Bad to the bone: what on earth for?

Baddest of the bad: the worst of the worst

Bailing out: reneging

Bait and switch: advertising an unavailable product as a come-on

Balance of nature: coordination

Bald before your time: less hairs to be counted and cared for

Ballpark figure: a rough estimate

Balls to the wall: an utmost effort

Bang-up job: superior workmanship

Baring your teeth: giving a warning

Barrel of laughs: the class clown

Based on a true story: right, tell me another one. "If prizes were given for lying, writers would win every time" (Ernest Hemingway).

Batten down the hatches: preparation for an impending storm

Battle hardened: worldly wise

Battle of ideas: freedom of speech, everyone and everything is fair game

Battle with the bottle: fighting loneliness and boredom

Be fair and square: deal straight from the deck

Be there or be square: attending a popular event

Be true to yourself: and the truth will set you free

Bear in mind: serve the greater need. It's right as rain.

Bear with me: sooner or later I'll get it right

Beat the devil: deliverance

Beauty is in the eye of the beholder: each individual has unique standards of beauty. "In life beauty perishes, not in art" (Leonardo DaVinci).

Beauty's only skin deep: true beauty comes from the heart and soul of a person. "Beauty is truth, truth beauty, that is all you know on Earth and all you need to know" (Percy Shelly).

Been around the block: an older person with experience who served every day of it

Been there before: it also happened to you. You know what they're going through.

Been there, done that: myriad experiences

Beg, borrow, or steal: you're determined to accomplish it by using all the means at your disposal

Beggars can't be choosers: asking for something, receiving it, and then complaining about it

Behind every cloud there's a silver lining: we learn from misfortunes

Behind the scenes: very private, admission by invitation only

Bend but don't break: perseverance

Bending over backwards: doing whatever you possibly can to assist someone

Bending your ear: listening to a blabbermouth

Bend swords into ploughshares: ending a quarrel

Best of both worlds: when you love what you're doing for a living. "And join both profit and delight into one" (Creech).

Better done than said: do it. Don't just talk about it.

Better late than never: at least you showed up

Better off dead: "Whoever loves this life will lose it" (New Testament).

Better off without it: something for nothing

Better safe than sorry: protecting yourself against possible harm

Better than nothing: what you already have

Better to err on the side of caution: double check it

Between the devil and the deep blue sea: burial at sea

Beware of Greeks bearing gifts: appearances can be deceptive. Things are not always as they seem, assume nothing.

Beyond reach: the truth. "Man can embody truth but he cannot know it" (William Butler Yeats).

Beyond the realm of possibilities: impossible. "The things which are impossible to man are possible to God" (New Testament).

Bide your time: wait until the right moment

Big bucks: lots of money

Big time: absolutely. By a wide margin. No doubt about it.

Bigger and better things: move on to them

Bigger fish to fry: more important things to do

Biggest bang for the buck: the best economic value

Biggest challenge of your life: risking your life to save a life. There's nothing greater one can do than this. "It's a far, far, better thing to do than you have ever done before" (Charles Dickens).

Bingo: hurrah!

Birds and the bees: everybody's doing it

Birds of a feather flock together: people tend to shop for the necessities of life in proximity to their homes

Bite the bullet: bear the pain

Bite the dust: don't ask for whom the siren sounds, it sounds for you

Bits and pieces: from here, there, and everywhere. "Everything is a father of remembrance" (William Shakespeare).

Black sheep: there is almost always one in a large family. "Oh, horrible, horrible, horrible" (William Shakespeare).

Blazing a trail: showing the way forward

Blessing in disguise: at first you did not know how good it was going to be. "We must laugh and we must sing, we are blessed by everything, everything we look upon is blessed" (William Butler Yeats).

Bless my soul: sighing. "Oh, Ireland, where Caesar and Christ go hand in hand" (James Joyce).

Blew your mind: fantastic

Blew your wad: spent

Blind, deaf, and dumb: resisting involvement

Bling bling: designer jewelry, a fashion statement

Blood, sweat, and tears: the birth and making of a country and a family. One comes from many.

Blow the whistle: turning someone in to the authorities for committing a crime against nature

Blow your top: losing your temper, not keeping it together

Blue collar workers: people who earn a living primarily with their hands

Bone of contention: an unresolved dispute

Boom or bust: all or nothing

Bored to death: disinterested

Born with a silver spoon in your mouth: some people are luckier than others

Borrowing from Peter to pay Paul: going from debt to worse debt

Bosom buddies: friends to the end

Bottoms up: finishing your drink

Bought and paid for: it's yours. You own it.

Bought it for a song: way below market value

Bounce it up: raise to the maximum

Bounce right back: "When in disgrace with fortune and men's eyes" (William Shakespeare).

Boxed in: no room to maneuver

Brains not brawn: much more has been accomplished with mind power than with muscle power

Brave the elements: go out and mingle with the crowd. "No man is an island entirely of himself" (John Donne).

Bread and butter: sustenance

Break the news: be the first to tell them about it. "The Son of Man comes at an hour when you think not" (New Testament).

Breathing down your neck: too close for comfort, nerve-racking

Breathing new life into it: mouth-to-mouth resuscitation

Bringing home the bacon: the principal moneymaker of a family

Bring the hammer down: confront them with force

Bring the house down: an overwhelming theatrical success, a smash hit

Brought something to the table: contributing substantially to the undertaking

Brown bagging it: carrying food with you

Brushed off: on the losing side of a broken love affair

Bucking the odds: the odds are highly unfavorable but you're going to attempt it anyway

Bucking the system: anti-establishment

Built like a brick shithouse: a woman with a buxom figure

Bundle of nerves: all tied up in knots

Burning a candle at both ends: wearing yourself out by overworking

Burning a hole in your pocket: money you want to spend

Burning the midnight oil: staying up very late at night to get the job done

Burst your bubble: cutting you down to size

Busted, disgusted, and can't be trusted: you're broke

Busting a gut: having a good laugh, hopefully the last laugh

Busy as a bee: staying active. "They polish life by useful arts" (Unknown).

Butterflies in your stomach: the forthcoming event has you filled with apprehension

Butting heads: accomplishing nothing through absolute disagreement

Buy cheap and sell dear: the essence of business

By any stretch of the imagination: it's impossible to comprehend

By hook or by crook: it's going to be done cleverly or illegally

By leaps and bounds: rapid growth

By the powers that be: those that have the most control over your life

Cake walk: little or no opposition

Call a spade a spade: speak your mind

Call it a day: stop working

Call it a night: time to go to home sweet home. "Be it ever so humble, there's no place like home" (Unknown).

Call it quits: take a break

Call off the dogs: stop the harassment

Call to arms: be there

Called on the carpet: being accused of something and then defending yourself

Calling each other names: trading insults

Calls the shots: the boss

Calm before the storm: feast or famine. The vicissitudes of life.

Calm in the eye of the storm: a steadfast soldier

Can carry a tune: a good singer

Can do no wrong: on a lucky streak

Can really shovel it down: a big eater

Can't back down: once you're in too far

Can't catch a cold: a total lack of luck

Can't get juice out of a turnip: don't try something that is impossible to do

Can't hold a candle to: when compared to someone engaged in the same type of activity, you're not even close to being as good as they are

Can't hold their liquor: a Dr. Jekyll and a Mr. Hyde

Can't make heads or tails of it: you don't understand it

Can't make it stick: insufficient evidence

Can't make up your mind: indecisive

Can't paint everyone with the same brush: like snowflakes and fingerprints, each individual is different. "Fashioned by the immanent will that stirs and urges everything" (Thomas Hardy).

Can't pull it out of thin air: it takes a lot of work

Can't see the forest for the trees: it was evident but somehow or another you did not see it because something clouded your mind. "Things fall apart, the center cannot hold. The best lack all conviction, while the worst are full of passionate intensity" (William Butler Yeats).

Can't walk and chew bubble gum at the same time: a complete idiot

Can't win for losing: if it wasn't for bad luck, you'd have no luck at all

Can't you get it through your head: why don't you understand it?

Capital gains: rolling assets over, avoiding taxation

Carried away: going overboard with it

Carries the load: your automobile, wheelchair, legs, walker, cane, etc.

Carrying the torch: continuing on with someone's work after they have passed away

Carry on: keep doing what you're doing, stay with it

Carry your own water: self-sufficient, looking out for yourself

Carry your own weight: do your share

Carve a niche: find a place for yourself

Cast a shadow over it: making it gloomy

Cat and mouse game: playing with your prey

Cat got your tongue: at a loss for words

Cat's meow: the best, the bee's knees

Catch them napping: then pounce and take advantage of them

Catches your eye: attractive, beautiful, out of the ordinary. "Where the path has lost its way, where the sun forgets the day" (John Clare).

Caught a case: a criminal indictment

Caught in the middle: not wanting to take sides. "To be or not to be" (William Shakespeare).

Caught with your hand in cookie jar: attempted theft

Caught with your pants down: totally surprised and unprepared. 9/11/01. "And death shall have no dominion" (Unknown).

Cause a scene: disturbing people with outrageous behavior

Cause for alarm: a hidden danger

Cave in: surrender

Center of attention: everybody wants to be it

Chalk it up: another success

Change of heart: reversing your point of view

Changing of the guard: the next generation taking over the reins of power from the previous one

Changing times: from B.C. to A.D.

Charmed life: damn lucky

Chasing the dragon: a user of opium

Check's in the mail: stalling for time to pay a bill

Chewing nails and spitting tacks: someone who is not as tough as they think they are

Chew them up and spit them out: defeat them soundly

Chicken shit: no heart. "Punks, just punks" (Jack Palance).

Chickens coming home to roost: right back at you

Chip off the old block: a person of high quality with great character

Chomping at the bit: impatient, raring to go

Chump change: not much money, peanuts

Class act: a gentleman and a scholar. A lovely lady. "For thee my tuneful accents will I raise, and treat of arts disclosed in ancient days" (John Dryden).

Clean as a whistle: spotless

Clean up your act: stop doing reprehensible things

Cleanliness is next to Godliness: with charity in your heart, you're something, without it, you're nothing

Clearing your name: vindication. "Repent what is past, avoid what is to come" (William Shakespeare).

Climbing the walls: very nervous, need a fix

Cloak and dagger: clandestine behavior

Close brush with death: the time in your life when you came close to being killed but were spared. A matter of life and death.

Close but no cigar: almost succeeding

Close call: It could have gone either way

Clothes make the man: the way a person dresses reveals how they want people to perceive them

Cloud of suspicion: it usually begins with ignorance. "We often grow to hate what we fear" (William Shakespeare).

Cock and bull story: lie upon lie, the runaround

Cool your heels: relax, take it easy

Come clean: don't lie, tell the truth

Come down to earth: flights of imagination have put your head in the clouds

Come hell or high water: the task at hand will be attempted no matter what obstacles may be in the way

Come on strong: persistent pursuit of a lady

Come to blows: an ultimatum

Comes up smelling like a rose: fortunate in spite of the circumstances

Comes with the territory: things you dislike

Coming apart at the seams: shattered nerves

Coming at you from both sides: caught in a crossfire

Coming into your own: reaching your full potential

Coming of age: maturing

Coming out of the woodwork: before there was hardly anyone, now they're everywhere

Coming out of your shell: interacting with people. No longer keeping to yourself.

Coming up in the world: progressing steadily

Complication at its worst: the I.R.S.

Complications of the heart: which one do you love the most?

Consider the consequences: rethink it

Consider the possibilities: how to properly play poker

Contrary to popular belief: "Technology has exceeded our humanity" (Albert Einstein).

Cooking something up: secretive planning

Cool as a cucumber: as cool as they come

Cool, calm, and collected: at peace with yourself

Cop a plea: beg for mercy

Cornered like a rat: zero alternatives

Costs an arm and a leg: a costly commodity

Costs a pretty penny: it's expensive

Cough it up: pay the money you owe

Could eat a horse: a voracious appetite

Could kick yourself in the ass: for not having done it when you had the chance

Couldn't fight his way out of a paper bag: a weakling

Couldn't hit the broad side of a barn: poor marksmanship

Couldn't put my finger on it: you could not figure it out

Count your blessings: each and every day

Count your lucky stars: for a narrow escape from danger. "A sadder but wiser man" (Samuel Coleridge).

Court of public opinion: it can make or break you

Cover all the bases: investigate all the possibilities concerning the matter. Leave no stone unturned.

Cover to cover: completely and thoroughly

Cover your ass: with plenty of backup

Cover your back: with eyes in the back of your head. Don't let anyone sneak up behind you and stab you in the back.

Crack the whip: show them who's boss

Cramping your style: by being with you

Crap shoot: anyone can win

Crawled out from under a rock: a despicable degenerate

Crazy like a fox: to mask your real intentions

Creature of habit: doing the same thing, day in, day out

Cross my fingers and hope to die: I'm not lying. Your word is your bond.

Cross over to the other side: passing away. "Nothing can bring back the hour, of splendor in the grass, of glory in the flower" (William Wordsworth).

Crossing the line: pushing it too far

Cruel and unusual punishment: driving in rush-hour traffic

Cry foul: when play is unfair

Cry me a river: stop complaining and whining

Crying poor: faking poverty for a handout

Curiosity killed the cat: not minding your own business can lead to disaster

Cut and dry: it's simple

Cut from the same cloth: identical traits in common

Cut off the head and the body can't function: ultimate strategy during war

Cut to the quick: make it short and sweet

Cut your losses: pull out before you lose everything

Cutting a rug: dancing

Cutting corners: sacrificing quality to complete a project sooner

Cutting it thin: economically depressed

Cutting someone down to size: making a big shot a little shot by outwitting them

Cutting your own throat: causing your own downfall

Damned if you do, damned if you don't: either way you lose

Dance circles around you: superior in every way

Dark horse: an unexpected contender

Day late and a dollar short: narrowly missing it

Dead bang: caught in the act

Dead men tell no tales: and best of all they can't bite

Dead on your feet: exhausted

Deal me out: I'm not participating

Deep six it: throw it away, get rid of it, eighty-six it

Defy gravity: become an astronaut

Defy the odds: make the wrong move at the right time

Delegation of authority: getting someone else to do your work

Devil of a time: painstakingly difficult

Diamond in the rough: the talent is there beneath the surface and has to be refined. A Cinderella waiting to emerge.

Diamonds are a girl's best friend: as long as they don't have to buy them

Diddly squat: zero, nothing, nada, zilch

Did you see what I saw?: unbelievable

Didn't bat an eye: unflappable

Didn't just drive up: experienced, seasoned

Didn't miss a beat: went smoothly, nothing went wrong

Die with your boots on: before you become dependent on others. "Dying is as natural as living" (Arthur Miller).

Different strokes for different folks: one person's pastime is of no interest to another

Dig it: knowing what it's about

Digging a ditch you can't get out of: reaching rock bottom and a point of no return

Digging it: fondness

Digging your own grave: your conduct is going to bring you down

Dime a dozen: a cheap commodity

Discretion is the greater part of valor: if you're prepared to go to the limit for a cause, make certain you're in the right

Divide and conquer: strategically spreading disunity. "I came not to bring peace but a sword" (New Testament).

Do a one-eighty: change your mind

Do it by the numbers: no variations

Do or die: acting fast during a life-threatening emergency

Do the math: figure it out

Do the right thing: treat others as you would like them to treat you, follow the Golden Rule

Do you need a medal or a chest to pin it on?: a medal is a vainglorious hook used by the military as an enticement. Old soldiers fade away, young ones get killed.

Do you need an open invitation?: it's obvious what you must do

Do your homework: be properly prepared, it pays off

Dodged a bullet: through some fortuitous act you did not become a victim. "Beasts of each kind their fellows spare, bear lives in amity with bear" (Decimus Juvenalis).

Does a bear shit in the woods?: of course

Does more harm than good: something for nothing, a handout

Doesn't have a leg to stand on: the argument put forth is not supported by sufficient evidence. "There is nothing a man will not believe in his favor" (Decimus Juvenalis).

Doesn't have two nickels to rub together: impecunious, not a pot to piss in. "Blessed are the poor" (New Testament).

Doesn't miss a thing: infallible

Doesn't sit well: it's disagreeable

Dog-eat-dog world: you have to look out for number one, self-preservation rules. "Man, once a slave, a dupe, a deceiver, a traveler from the cradle to the grave" (Percy Shelly).

Dogging someone: displaying a threatening posture towards a person

Doing time: incarcerated. "The vilest deeds, like poison weeds, bloom well in prison air, and all that's good in man wastes and withers there" (Richard Lovelace).

Domino effect: when one topples, others topple with it

Don't air your dirty laundry in public: avoid idle gossip. "Let them have it how they will! You are tired, best be still" (Matthew Arnold).

Don't ask me how I did it: fortune smiled upon me, serendipity

Don't beat a dead horse: don't do it if it serves no purpose whatsoever

Don't beat around the bush: come directly to the point

Don't believe everything you hear: beware of propaganda and compulsive liars

Don't bite the hand that feeds you: do not reciprocate a good turn with ingratitude

Don't bug me: stop annoying me

Don't call me, I'll call you: avoiding a numbskull

Don't chance it: too risky. "Beer after whiskey, very risky, whiskey after beer, never fear" (Unknown).

Don't change horses in midstream: if you have a good thing going, keep it as it is

Don't count me out: I'm still here, standing tall

Don't count on it: it probably won't happen

Don't count your chickens before they hatch: wait until it's over before there's cause for celebration

Don't cross the bridge until you come to it: don't do it until it must be done. Put it off today because it can be done tomorrow.

Don't cry over spilled milk: save your tears for something more serious than a minor misfortune

Don't cry wolf: never dial 911 unless it's an emergency

Don't cut off your nose to spite your face: don't do anything rash that can't be undone. You may or may not live to regret it.

Don't do this to me: use and abuse

Don't drop the ball: when assigned to do a job, do it right

Don't go there: topic is off limits

Don't fall for it: a practical joke

Don't fence me in: give me some room

Don't hold your breath: it will never happen

Don't jump the gun: start at the right time

Don't kiss and tell: keep your sex life private

Don't know what the story is: not knowing the facts that are causing the problem

Don't know whether they're coming or going: perplexed

Don't know your ass from a hole in the ground: dim-witted, a simpleton

Don't let the world pass you by: become a part of it

Don't look a gift horse in the mouth: accept a present without complaint

Don't look back: always forward

Don't lose your cool: calm yourself down

Don't make a federal case out of it: it's no big deal

Don't press your luck: you're beginning to make me mad

Don't put all your eggs into one basket: diversify with respect to all aspects of your life

Don't quit your day job: your other field of endeavor may not pan out

Don't rain on my parade: don't make a mess out of my life

Don't rock the boat: never doing this makes you an absolute conformist

Don't sell yourself cheap: charge top dollar for your time and effort. "The laborer is worthy of his hire" (New Testament).

Don't show all your cards: sometimes it's beneficial to do this when negotiating a business deal

Don't sink to their level: adhere to a virtuous model of conduct

Don't that beat all: an unusual occurrence

Don't throw stones at glass houses: always respect the handicapped, you might be in the same boat someday

Don't throw the baby out with the bath water: be careful and pay attention

Don't turn the other cheek: defend yourself and your family from harm

Don't want to put you on the spot: placing a friend in a position they may not want to be in

Dot the i's and cross the t's: do it carefully with attention to detail

Double-edged sword: it harms you, no matter what side you're on

Double standard: advocating a way to behave but not adhering to it

Double talk: not coming directly to the point, talking in circles

Double whammy: two strikes against you right off the bat

Down and dirty: the nitty-gritty

Down but not out: you still have a slight chance, stay with it

Down in the dumps: feeling blue, depressed

Down in the trenches: doing the dirty work

Down the road: it will be available soon. "The peace which passes understanding" (David Lawrence).

Down-to-earth person: no pretensions, can mix and mingle anywhere

Dragging their feet: deliberately delaying what needs to be done

Dragging your tail: tired, low energy level

Dream without boundaries: anything is possible

Dressed to kill: going to a funeral or a wedding

Dressed to the nines: got on your best clothes and are looking good

Driving you to drink: rattling your nerves

Drop a dime on someone: becoming a stoolpigeon, snitch, informer

Dropped the ball: a major mistake, you blew it

Dropping a line: communication

Dropping like flies: when you are near or at old age, friends and acquaintances die frequently

Drown your sorrows: getting drunk to the point of forgetfulness

Drummed into your head: teaching by repetition

Earned your money the new-fashioned way: you sued for it

Earth-shattering news: stop the presses!

Easier said than done: it may be above and beyond your capacity

Easy come, easy go: all that you had, have, and will have. "Trust on and hope tomorrow will repay, tomorrow's falser than the former day" (John Dryden).

Easy money: winning a big jackpot gambling

Eat your heart out: a term used to evoke envy

Eaten alive: overpowered by a wide margin

Eating out of the palm of your hand: you got them where you want them

Egg on your face: making a fool out of yourself

Egging you on: baiting you to get you upset

Either or: one or the other

End of story: you don't wish to discuss it anymore

Error of your ways: not knowing the difference between right and wrong

Even Steven: you don't owe me and I don't owe you

Every dog has its day: everyone has, at one time in their life, had a day when they felt on top of the world

Every hair on your head is counted: all that you think and do is recorded

Every man for himself: this could justifiably occur during a natural disaster

Every name in the book: you must have called someone this more than once

Everybody needs somebody: it's too tough to go it alone

Everyone and their brother: too many people know about it. It's been done too often. It's too crowded.

Everyone goes their own way: alone we enter into life and alone we depart from it. "Scorn the multitude, alive and dead" (John Dryden).

Everyone has skeletons in their closet: we have all done something we were ashamed of. A sinner among sinners.

Everyone has their faults: nobody's perfect

Everyone has their price: I don't think so. Some people can't be bought.

Everything is relative: everything is dependent upon each other

Everything's coming up roses: very pleasant things are happening. There's nothing to complain about.

Everything's peachy: in a good frame of mind

Everything to gain and nothing to lose: so why not do it?

Everything under the sun: and over and around it

Every way but sideways: enter and exit. "The whole world is a stage" (William Shakespeare).

Every which way but loose: sexual intercourse

Excuse my French: pardon me for blurting out an obscenity

Eyes are the windows to the soul: a person's eyes reveal what they have experienced. "Our eyes see clearly only after they have been washed with tears" (Unknown).

Eyes in the back of your head: a keen sense of perception

Eye to eye: a straight-forward discussion

Face the music: confess, pay for the consequences of your actions

Fact of the matter is: no one has a clue about what's really happening

Failure to communicate: eyes that do not see and ears that do not hear

Fair trade: don't cheat. "Give full measure and weigh with even scales" (Koran).

Fall guy: solely taking the blame for an offense when others were just as culpable

Fame is fleeting: celebrities come and celebrities go

Far be it for us to understand: the universe. "The truth is immaterial" (Eugene O'Neil).

Fasten your seatbelts: get ready for a shock

Fat chance: it will never happen

Fate is fickle: each day we all have to play the hand we're dealt. "On fickle wings the minutes haste, and fortunes favors never last" (Unknown).

Fate worse than death: discovering the Fountain of Youth and living an interminable length of time. "All things ripen, fall, and cease, to dark death or dreamful ease" (Alfred Tennyson).

Feel like a bump on a log: a place where you feel out of place

Feel them out: to see what they're up to

Feeling between mystery and hope: hanging in there

Feeling your oats: strong and vigorous

Fell flat on your face: abysmal failure

Few and far between: extraordinary good luck

Fight fire with fire: give at least as good as you're getting

Fighting a losing battle: no matter what you do, you can't win

Fighting the good fight: defending the defenseless

Figment of your imagination: that you're above it all

Final nail in your coffin: rest in peace

Finders keepers, losers weepers: it belongs to me now

Finer things in life: peace with comfort

First among equals: the best of your kind

First and foremost: the main reason

First the carrot, then the stick: how to properly court a woman

First things first: do the most important chore first

Fish them in: taking advantage of suckers. "There's one born every minute" (P.T. Barnum).

Fit as a fiddle: in fine physical condition

Fit for neither man nor beast: inclement weather

Five will get you ten: giving two-to-one odds on a bet

Flea markets: bizarre bazaars

Fly-by-night outfit: a business that cons people out of money without performing and disappears

Flying by the seat of your pants: doing it for the first time without preparation

Flying off the handle: losing your temper, becoming unglued

Flying off the shelf: selling rapidly

Follow in your father's footsteps: "Imitation is the highest form of flattery" (Unknown).

Follow it to a tee: don't change the blueprint

Follow your star: discover your destiny

Fool's paradise: rich people squandering natural resources. "Verily, they will have their comeuppance" (New Testament).

Fools rush in: the wise ponder

Fooling around: having sex

Foot loose and fancy free: not tied to anyone or anything, a free spirit

Foot the bill: paying for everything

For all intents and purposes: "Love does various minds does variously inspire, it stirs in gentle bosoms gentle fire" (John Dryden).

For all the marbles: your whole stake, all in

For better or worse: "In youth and beauty, wisdom is so rare" (William Shakespeare).

Force of habit: irresistible

Full of shit: can't deliver the goods

Full plate: much work to do

Fun-filled day: when everything goes your way

Gaining ground: what wars are for. "And claim as a soldier's right, a charter to commit the crime once more" (William Butler Yeats).

Gay lingo: sissy speak

Get a grip on yourself: pull yourself together, stop acting like an idiot

Get a leg up on them: an advantage

Get a life: start doing something useful

Get away from it all: take a vacation to a faraway place

Get down to the nitty-gritty: the true substance of the matter

Get in line: everyone likes it

Get in on the act: a strong desire to participate

Get it off your chest: tell someone about it

Get my drift: do you know what I'm talking about?

Get off your high horse: stop thinking you're better than everyone else

Get on the ball: stop daydreaming and try to make all the right moves

Get on the horn: make a telephone call

Get out of Dodge: leaving the place you're presently living at because of intolerable conditions

Get out while the getting's good: before it's too late

Get over it: any misfortune

Get real: stop being a phony

Get-rich-quick schemes: both sides of internet gambling, the players and the websites

Get serious: time to wake up

Get the show on the road: start moving

Get the wax out of your ears: listen and pay attention

Get the word out: inform people about an exciting upcoming event

Get to the point: "Brevity is the soul of wit" (Unknown).

Get up to snuff: as good as you can be

Get used to it: growing older. "An aged man is but a paltry thing, a tattered coat upon a stick, unless soul claps its hands and sings" (William Butler Yeats).

Get with it: be part of the team

Get with the program: fall into line, cooperate

Get your dander up: outraged

Get your feet back on the ground: stop thinking you're so high and mighty

Get your foot in the door: to begin a good beginning

Get your head together: stop being a fool

Get your mind out of the gutter: aspire to higher thoughts. "Nor love thy life, nor hate, but while you live, live well, how long or short, permit to heaven" (John Milton).

Getting a rise out of you: a hooker plying her trade

Getting back on track: finding the groove again

Getting bug-eyed: suffering an eye strain

Getting carried away: overdoing it

Getting clipped: swindled. In modern parlance, ripped off.

Getting cold feet: disinterest replacing enthusiasm

Getting down and dirty: a leader in the trenches with subordinates

Getting hot under the collar: becoming mad slowly but surely

Getting in your face: intimidation. "Hell itself is my only foe" (John Clare).

Getting on your case: ridiculing, ragging on you

Getting out of hand: rowdiness

Getting out of line: unruly, behaving badly

Getting out from under their shadow: by your own merit

Getting over on someone: fooling them by putting them on

Getting paid under the table: avoiding taxation

Getting the hang of it: becoming proficient

Getting to the bottom of it: investigating to find the truth of the matter, digging into it

Getting your ducks in a row: becoming well-organized. "So in your veins red life might stream again" (Percy Shelly).

Getting your rocks off: having an orgasm

Ghost of a chance: none at all

Give and take: mixing it up

Give it all you got: and then some

Give it a rest: I'm tired of hearing about it

Give it a shot: try it, you might like it

Give me a break: quit picking on me, cut me some slack

Give me liberty or give me death: sometimes you have to put your life on the line. "The tree of liberty is soaked with the blood of patriots" (Thomas Paine).

Give someone a fighting chance: be a good sport

Give the devil its due: no one can be all bad, not even the devil itself

Give them an inch and they'll take a mile: give someone something for nothing, and they may take kindness for weakness and try to take all that you have

Give them a taste: a small sample

Give them enough rope and they'll hang themselves: profit by their mistakes

Giving away the store: making deals that render no profit

Giving someone the benefit of doubt: don't judge anyone. "Who made the heart, he alone decidedly can try us" (Robert Burns).

Giving someone the business: making fun of them

Given the green light: the go ahead, permission granted

Given the third degree: an unrelenting interrogation

Giver not a taker: someone who cares about the whole, not just one of the parts. "He gave his life as a ransom for many" (New Testament).

Glutton for punishment: masochistic tendencies

Go by the book: that's why it was written

Go down fighting: if at all possible, never let someone bind and gag you

Go fly a kite: get lost, beat it

Go for broke: risk everything

Go for the gusto: top prize, first place

Go for the jugular: find the weak spot and show no mercy and take no prisoners. "An eagle towering in his pride of place, was by a mousing owl, hawked at and killed" (William Shakespeare).

Go over their head: when dealing with bureaucrats who ignore you

Go the distance: finish what you started, don't be a quitter

Go toe to toe: slug it out

Go to the blazes: hell

Go with the flow: fitting in. "To make a happy fireside clime to weans and wife, that's the true pathos and sublime of human life" (Robert Burns).

Gobble it up: fine knowledge

God help us: we all need it

God helps them who help themselves: it's there for the taking. "What female heart can gold despise? What cat's averse to fish?" (Richard Grey).

God's gift to: conceited

God works in mysterious ways: and we can only guess at the motives. "There's a divinity that shapes our ends, rough hew them how we will" (William Shakespeare).

Godspeed: good luck, take care, be careful. "There is a necessity in fate where the brave bold man is fortunate" (John Dryden).

Going against the grain: taking the road that's less traveled. "I hail the superhuman, I call it death in life, and life in death" (William Butler Yeats).

Going around in circles: accomplishing nothing

Going belly up: out of business, bankrupt. "You have to be willing to fail in order to succeed" (John Barrymore).

Going cold turkey: quitting a bad habit suddenly

Going down in flames: failing totally, no chance for recovery

Going full circle: you're right back where you started from

Going gently into the good night: dying in your sleep. "To bear the ills we have and fly to others we know not of" (William Shakespeare).

Going great guns: putting forth an utmost effort

Going native: adaptation of the species

Going nowhere fast: incompetence at its worst, spinning your wheels

Going out in style: finishing with a flourish

Going out on a limb: taking a risk

Going out in a blaze of glory: supremely bringing something to an end

Going the extra mile: doing as much as you can do

Going through the motions: your heart's not in it

Going through the roof: skyrocketing prices, gigantic inflation

Going too far: impolite

Going underground: hiding out, on the run from the law

Going under the knife: having your body cut open during a medical operation

Gone to seed: letting yourself go

Good chemistry: mutual respect, agreeably working together

Good for nothing: some people. "To be choked with hate, may well be of all evil chances chief" (William Butler Yeats).

Good intentions can harm you: although they sincerely tried to help you, the result is often harmful

Good people: nice, friendly, courteous, tolerant

Good run for your money: you lost money gambling but had fun and came close to winning

Good sleeping weather: a nice cool evening

Good things come to those who wait: "Adopt the pace of nature, her pace is patience" (Budda).

Good to the last drop: fine liquor

Goody Two-shoes: a prude

Got it written all over you: it's apparent

Got religion: holier than thou. "Poetry will replace religion" (Matthew Arnold).

Got the goods on you: sufficient evidence

Got them where you want them: in a compromising position

Got tied up: unexpectedly delayed

Got what's coming to you: payback. "What lives once, lives forever" (Budda).

Got you by the balls: you must consent

Got you coming and going: you can't win

Got you over a barrel: doing it a different way would not be worth the time and effort

Got you pegged: knowing what you're really like

Got your clock cleaned: your ass was kicked

Grab the bull by the horns: take on the task immediately with all your might

Grasping at straws: repeatedly trying when you should stop because it's helpless

Greasing palms: bribery

Great day in the morning: it's wonderful to be alive

Great expectations: pipe dreams. "Cast a cold eye on life, on death, horseman pass by" (William Butler Yeats).

Grin and bear it: no matter how bad things are, don't sink to the level of despair. "His outward smiles concealed his inward grief" (John Dryden).

Growing old gracefully: the aging process is a changing course set by nature in stages. "Grow old along with me, the best is yet to be" (Robert Browning).

Guilty as sin: all of us. "We cannot assert the innocence of anyone, whereas we can state with certainty the guilt of all" (Albert Camus).

Guilty pleasure: it's bad for your health, but you can't resist it

Gun control: "Never trust a government that doesn't trust its citizens with guns"(Thomas Jefferson).

Gun shy: running scared, timid

Gut instinct: go with it

Had it out: settled an argument

Had the rug pulled out from under you: left breathless. "When shall the stars be blown about the sky, like the sparks blown out of a smithy, and lie" (William Butler Yeats).

Had your time in the sun: the good times are gone. "You've had your share of laughter, food, and drink, it's time to quit the scene, it's time to think" (Elphinson).

Hair of the dog that bit you: drinking the same alcoholic beverage you drank the night before to cure a hangover

Hair trigger: easily set off

Half-baked plan: poorly drawn

Ham it up: over-performing when in the spotlight

Hammered: befuddled, imbibed too much

Hand in hand: together, side by side

Hand-to-mouth existence: barely surviving

Handed to you on a silver platter: serendipitous opportunity

Handle it with kid gloves: treat it gently and with great care

Hands are full: very busy, a multitude of tasks to complete

Hands are tied: powerless to remedy the situation

Handsome as a devil: the devil in disguise

Handsome is as handsome does: being handsome has its advantages

Hang in there: don't give up

Hang loose: I'll return soon with what you need

Hang tough: stick with it

Hanging loose like a Mother Goose: calmly waiting for instructions or somebody

Hanging on by a thread: position precarious

Hanging on for dear life: close to a total collapse. "Some soothing thoughts spring out of human suffering" (William Wordsworth).

Hangups: dislikes, prejudices

Hard act to follow: a life many would like to emulate but very few, if any, can

Hard to put down: a good book

Has a chip on his shoulder: a bad attitude

Has a mind of its own: it won't stop

Has a screw loose: a mental disease. "Canst thou minister to a mind diseased. Pluck from the memory a rooted sorrow. Raze out the written troubles of the mind" (William Shakespeare).

Has a set of balls: a macho man

Hash it out: give and take to resolve the problem

Hasn't hit you yet: the full effect

Hats off: a gesture of admiration

Have a bone to pick: confronting someone who did you dirty

Have a crush on someone: temporarily infatuated

Have a good one: wishing someone a pleasant day

Have a heart: be merciful, show some compassion

Have all the time in the world: positively patient

Have a lock on it: monopolization

Have an axe to grind: waiting to get even. Disregarding vengeance is the "weakest frailty of a feeble mind" (John Dryden).

Have and have nots: plunderers and the desperate

Have a score to settle: preparing for a day of reckoning

Have bigger fish to fry: more important things to attend to

Have friends in high places: the right connections

Have it down to a science: precision

Have some gas left: you can still go some, bring it on

Have the drop on you: an indefensible position

Have the hots for: romantically inclined

Have the runs: diarrhea, nature calls

Have to live with it: all that has transpired thus far in your life

Haven't got a hair on your ass: shrinking from taking risks or gambles

Having a bad hair day: things aren't going well

Having a field day with it: discussing it with great enthusiasm

Having game: willing to take a chance. "The harvest is great but the laborers are few" (New Testament).

Having nothing but time: willing to wait

Having someone in your back pocket: complete control over them

Having the last laugh: in the end you were victorious

Having the skinny: allegedly possessing the true facts about a topic of gossip

He who hesitates is lost: seize the moment and disregard "haste makes waste" (Unknown).

Head and shoulders above the rest: much better than those in the same group

Head over heels: hopelessly in love

Heads up: look out!

Healthy as a horse: physically fit. "Men should be as they seem" (William Shakespeare).

Heard it from the horse's mouth: it's not hearsay, you were there when it was said

Heard it through the grapevine: uncertain about who started the rumor

Heart of gold: they will give the shirt off their back to help someone in distress

Heavens to Betsy: exclaim this when upset or astonished

Heinz 57: mixed nationalities or races, a mutt

Hell hath no fury like a woman scorned: women are not the weaker sex

Hell on wheels: a real go-getter

Here goes nothing: it just might work

Here today, gone tomorrow: some things never last long. "In the long run we're all dead" (Ralph Emerson).

Here we go again: we've heard it all before

Here you go: a remittance

Hide and go seek: sin and then repent

High as a kite: feeling no pain due to substance abuse

High roller, big spender, living large: throwing money away. "A fool and his money are soon parted" (William Shakespeare).

High society: the effete elite, twigs in ivory towers

High tail it: move fast

His bark is worse than his bite: a loudmouth always shooting his mouth off. They talk the talk but don't walk the walk.

History in the making: world historical events

Hit all the right buttons: doing everything correctly. "He who many a year with toil of breath, found death in life, may find life in death" (William Wordsworth).

Hit-and-miss approach: using a high volume of product in business. The ones that sell big make up for the ones that fail.

Hit it off: quickly becoming friends with someone recently met. "Think where man's glory most begins and ends, and say, my glory was, I had such friends" (William Butler Yeats).

Hit on all cylinders: give it all you got

Hit pay dirt: striking it rich

Hit the bricks: get out of here

Hit the hay: it's bedtime

Hit the road: get lost

Hitting a brick wall: can't do any better or go further with it

Hitting it off: reciprocated feelings of goodwill

Hitting the skids: on the dole

Hold on to what you got: common sense

Hold on to your hat: something exciting is about to happen

Hold their hand: assist them step by step

Hold your horses: slow down

Hold your tongue: be quiet

Holding down the fort: looking after someone's home while they're away

Holding your own: you're at least as good as anyone else

Home away from home: It feels like home but isn't

Home cooking and health food: overrated

Honest to God: I'm telling the truth

Honesty is the best policy: "The Irish are an honest people, they don't have anything good to say about anyone" (Samuel Johnson).

Hook me up: get me what I want

Hop, skip, and a jump: nearby

Hope and faith: nourishment for the soul

Hope springs eternal: having faith. "A vision of eternity is the only excuse for remaining alive" (Samuel Beckett).

Horse of a different color: it's the same thing, but at first glance appears not to be

Hot and bothered: upset or sexually aroused

Hot on your heels: right behind you, trying to catch you

House of cards: a weak foundation, easily toppled

How does your garden grow?: by photosynthesis

How do you like them apples?: touche!

How low can you go?: until there's no turning back

How to live to a ripe old age: hard liquor and soft women

How to save humanity from itself: by working for the common cause

Human rights versus property rights: some make the bread and some just eat it

Humor me: tell me a story, fact or fiction

Hurry up and wait: just in time for a doctor's appointment

I ain't dead yet: "I have many miles to go before I sleep" (Robert Frost).

I am what I am: and you are what you are. "For all the accommodations you bear are nursed by baseness" (William Shakespeare).

I can read you like a book: you can't bullshit me

I can take a hint: say no more, I'm out of here, gone

I can't help myself: an addiction

I don't know you from Adam: a humorous way to say you never met someone before

I gathered that: I know what you're driving at

I get the picture: knowing what's happening

I get your point: cognition

I just died and went to heaven: exquisite delight

I know it and you know it: there's no room for argument

I know the feeling: I've been there before

I know where you live: an implied threat

I may be right or I may be wrong: does it really matter?

I never knew it was going to come to this: you end up where you are

I rest my case: my argument is over

I shit you not: it's the truth

I smell a rat: it's suspicious

I take it back: what I just said, pardon me

I thought I was going to have a baby: waiting a long time

I told you so: I warned you in advance

I trust you as far as I can throw you: jokingly said in reply to someone who asserts how trustworthy they are

I want to but I can't: it's against my religion

I wouldn't touch it with a ten-foot pole: it's that abhorrent

I would stake my life on it: supreme confidence

Idle hands are the devil's tools: stay active, otherwise, the devil's going to get you

If I didn't see it, I wouldn't have believed it: man landing on the moon

If it ain't broke, don't fix it: some things are better off as they are, leave well enough alone. "Striving to better often we mar what's well" (William Shakespeare).

If I told you once, I told you a thousand times: stop it

If it's broke, fix it: sometimes a change of attitude is good. "Show pity to the humbled soul, and crush the sons of pride" (Virgil).

If it's good enough for me, then it's good enough for you: don't be so picky, you nitpicker

If it's not one thing, it's another: that irritates you

If looks could kill: sometimes this is all it takes

If push comes to shove: stand your ground. "I strove with none, for none was worth my strife" (Walter Lander).

If the shoe fits, wear it: don't deny a true accusation

If the truth be known: we would all be saints. "You can refute the philosopher, but not the saint or the song of sixpence" (William Butler Yeats).

If you can't stand the heat, get out of the kitchen: if you can't do it, don't try to

If you don't like it, you can lump it: if you dislike me or what I'm doing, frankly, I don't give a damn

If you got it, flaunt it: shine your light

If you gotta go, you gotta go: relieving yourself

If you have an itch, scratch it: make it go away

If you live by the sword, you'll die by the sword: it remains to be seen if they started it

If you play with fire, you might get burnt: a dangerous but unnecessary act is foolhardy at best

If you've seen one, you've seen them all: not absolutely identical but close to it, like pornography

If you want to play, you have to pay: "One man's profit is another man's loss" (Unknown).

Ignorance is bliss: the more you know, the less you understand

I'll be a monkey's uncle: if it's true, and you thought otherwise, then this is what you are

I'll be damned if I know: the future. "Who knows if heaven with ever bounteous power, will add tomorrow to the present hour" (Francis).

I'll believe it when I see it: the Second Coming

I'll fix your wagon: retribution

I'll never hear the end of it: someone telling you the same story over and over

I'll never tell: I can keep a secret

I'll show you who's boss: displaying exceptional leadership ability

I'll take your word for it: I trust you

I'm all ears: prepared to listen

I'm from Missouri: I have to see it to believe it, show me

I'm hip: I know what you mean

I'm in seventh heaven: bountiful bliss

I'm my brother's keeper: if needs be, and my sister's too

I'm not going there: I don't want to talk about that

I'm not going to mention any names: granting anonymity to those you are going to put down

I'm not the one to talk: having the same fault in common

In a heartbeat: immediately, in a New York minute

In a league of your own: very special, one in two million

In a pinch: doing it only if you must. "A person is the origin of their actions" (Aristotle).

In bed with them: coconspirators

In cahoots: collusion

In deep shit: very serious trouble

In every way, shape, and form: a vivid description

In for a penny, in for a pound: strive to do your best by giving it your all. "Whatever you find your hand doing, do it with all your might" (Bible).

In hot water: facing an indictment

In like Flynn: a real lady killer

In many guises: how to write well

In my mind's eye: the way I look at things

In or out: for or against

In perfect harmony: "The soul and source of music, which reveals eternal harmony" (George Byron).

In the beginning: let there be light

In the black: making money

In the driver's seat: control

In the final analysis: "Rain falls on the just and the unjust" (New Testament).

In the grand scheme of things: "Life is like a walking shadow, where a poor player struts and frets his hour upon the stage, and then is heard no more" (William Shakespeare).

In the moment: truly alive, real

In the nick of time: there when desperately needed, just made it

In the old days: some were the same, some were different, but machines were absent

In the prime of life: you have never felt better in your life. "Now is not the winter of your discontent" (William Shakespeare).

In the red: losing money

In the right place at the right time: perfect timing

In the woods: any remote place

In the wrong place at the wrong place: applicable to anyone who has been a victim

In the zone: an athlete at their best

In this day and age: the present

In tip-top shape: prime physical condition

In way over your head: now you can't get out when you should

In your corner: on your side

In your cups: drunk and feeling no remorse. "When such as I cast out remorse so great a sweetness flows into my breast" (William Butler Yeats).

In your digs: at home

In your grave before your time: unattained longevity. Not, "withered, old, and skeleton gaunt" (William Butler Yeats).

In your hearts of hearts: what do you believe, what do you know, what are you really like?

In your own world: preoccupied

Inherit the wind: be free and worry not whenever you go to and come from a place

Invasion of privacy: someone sticking their nose in where it doesn't belong

Irish sports pages: the obituaries

Iron it out: come to an agreement

It ain't over until the fat lady sings: if she can sing

It all boils down to: becoming part and parcel of infinity

It beats the hell out of me: I haven't got the faintest idea

It becomes second nature: doing it automatically

It comes and it goes: inspiration and Lady Luck

It costs a pretty penny: very expensive

It crossed your mind: you thought about it momentarily

It didn't pan out: an unsuccessful venture

It doesn't add up: senseless, like history

It doesn't cost a dime: it's free

It doesn't ring a bell: I can't recall it

It don't mean nothing: a double negative emphasizing insignificance

It escapes me: I can't recall it at this moment

It goes without saying: understood without words

It never crossed my mind: not giving it a thought

It should be a breeze: easily done

It slipped my mind: you forgot about something and then recalled it later. My, how time flies.

It smells fishy: something just doesn't seem right

It spread like wildfire: out of control

It stinks to high heaven: a deal with terrible terms

It sucks: you hate it

It takes all kinds: world population

It takes money to make money: "Never ventured, never gained" (Unknown).

It takes one to know one: animals do it by sight, sound, smell, and touch. "I think, therefore I am" (Rene Descartes).

It was better before: than it is now. The boob tube is the main cause. "The mental disease of the present generation is impatience of study" (Samuel Johnson).

It was so funny I forgot to laugh: a bad joke

It went in one ear and out the other: you heard it but due to a lapse of attention you failed to retain it

It will all blow over: the public has a short memory

It will all come out in the wash: you can't hide anything. God is watching and keeping track of you. "From above to look below on humankind, bewildered in the maze of life and blind" (John Dryden).

It will make or break you: a harsh winter. "And vagrant nature bounds upon her prey" (Francis).

It won't go away: an irksome nagging mess

It'll make a man out of you: a very strenuous activity

It's about time: a lawsuit settlement

It's a crying shame: what guns are doing to our society

It's a free country: and your amount of freedom is based upon your bank book balance

It's a jungle out there: full of violence, asphalt, concrete, automobiles, sirens, oversized buildings, and people with nothing to lose

It's all over but the crying: you lost, loser

It's all the same in the dark: sex

It's all the same in the end: "Alas, it is delusion all, the future cheats us from afar, we can not be what we recall, nor dare we think on what we are" (George Byron).

It's a long story: one I do not wish to tell

It's always later than you think: until the end of time

It's a no-brainer: a simple thing to do

It's a sad story but true: every adult life is, for the most part, a tale of woe. "I know my life's a pain and but a span, and I know myself a proud yet wretched man" (John Davies).

It's a small world: and getting smaller with every population increase, to a possible point of no return, not heeding the law of diminishing returns

It's beside the point: it doesn't matter

It's beyond me: I don't know

It's closer than you think: the hereafter. "She died and left to me, this health, this calm and quiet scene, the memory of what has been and never more will be" (William Wordsworth).

It's cool: likeably nice

It's far from over: all this, that, and what's in between

It's fifty-fifty: it has an equal chance of succeeding or not succeeding

It's for me to know and for you to find out: I'm not going to reveal it

It's for real: not fake, the real McCoy

It's for the birds: you don't want anything to do with it

It's farther down the road: something to do at a later time. "The rarer action is in virtue than in vengeance" (William Shakespeare).

It's Greek to me: unintelligible

It's just a matter of time: before it will happen

It's just around the corner: the grim reaper with the answer to the question everyone asks themselves. "A riddle and a mystery wrapped in an enigma" (Winston Churchill).

It's late in the game: start now or you will miss your chance. "All are called but few are selected" (New Testament).

It's later than you think: change and you might be redeemed. Life is a test. Will you pass or fail?

It's like an open book: waiting to be known. "Read into the book of life" (Arthur Schopenhauer).

It's like music to my ears: any sound that pleases you. "Without music, life would be a mistake" (Friedrich Nietzsche).

It's like riding a bike: once you learn how to do it, you can still do it, despite not having done it for a long time

It's never too late: to beg for forgiveness. Humble yourself.

It's no big thing: don't be alarmed

It's no joke: I kid you not, it's for real

It's not over until it's over: keep playing the game with all your heart until the end

It's not the first time and it won't be the last time: when something good or bad happens. "The sun shines on both the good and the evil" (Bible).

It's not the heat, it's the humidity: the cause is underlying

It's now or never: do it

It's on your head: the guilt

It's out of the question: I won't do it

It's on me: I'll pay for it

It's pretty slick: done with imagination, creative

It's purely academic: you can discuss it but can no longer do it, for example, sex

It's so thick you could cut it with a knife: the humidity

It's the rule, not the exception: struggling through life

It's time to step down: retire and enjoy the fruits of your labor

It's too much: you can't take it anymore

It's too rich for my blood: you can't afford to gamble at such high stakes

It's touch and go: the outcome is uncertain, it could go either way

It's tough to take: bad news

It's up in the air: still undecided

It's up to you: the burden rests on your shoulders

It's written: the law

Jailbait: a promiscuous pretty girl under the age of consent, statutory rape

Jesus Christ: generally expressed to denote astonishment, confusion, emphasis, anger, wonder, sadness, happiness

Jewel of the crown: magnificence

Jockeying for position: a tactical move for an advantage

Johnny come lately: copying a good thing, copycat

Join the club: all in it together, willing or unwilling

Judge, jury, and executioner: a soldier engaged in guerilla warfare. "Only the dead have seen the end of war" (Plato).

Judgment call: think about it and then make your best decision

Jump at the chance: seize the opportunity, eager beaver

Jump on the bandwagon: joining because it's a good thing to be in on. "Happy for those who are of the fold" (Percy Shelly).

Jumped ship: went elsewhere

Jumping to conclusions: forming an opinion without knowing all the facts. When you do this, more often than not, you're far from correct.

Jury's still out: a definite decision or answer has not been rendered

Just another one of those days: when nothing goes right. It could be worse.

Just getting warmed up: to perform exceedingly well

Just like clockwork: same time, same place, same thing

Just like downtown: it's A OK

Just like that: you're up and then you're down

Just scratching the surface: a cursory preliminary inquiry

Just what the doctor ordered: a pure heart is the prescription to fill. "No physician delights in the health of their patients" (Moliere).

Justice for all: who are rich. The "just us" system.

K

Keel over: dropping dead suddenly

Keep a lid on it: don't disclose it

Keep a stiff upper lip: be brave, courageous, and bold

Keep close during a storm: it may be too dangerous to venture outside. "How sweet in sleep to pass the careless hours, lulled by the beating winds and dashing showers" (Unknown).

Keep doing what you're doing: if it works for you

Keep it to yourself: don't tell anyone about it

Keep it under your hat: do not reveal it

Keep it up: and you'll be sorry

Keep me posted: let me know what's going on from time to time

Keep plugging away: if at first you don't succeed, try and try again. "For they can conquer who believe they can" (John Dryden).

Keep the door open: maintain an open mind and "open your hand and satisfy every living thing with favor" (Talmud).

Keep them honest: call their bluff

Keep your cool: hold your temper, don't lose your head

Keep your eye on the ball: be "far out" by imagining you're in outer space observing the rotation of the Earth

Keep your eyes peeled: be on the lookout

Keep your feet back on the ground: affability

Keep your guard up: stay alert at all times

Keep your hand in: practice your craft

Keep your hands to yourself: do not touch

Keep your head on your shoulders: look before you leap

Keep your nose clean: stay out of trouble

Keep your powder dry: don't let provisions set aside for emergency purposes become useless

Keep yourself to yourself: mind your own business

Keeping up with the Joneses: trying to outdo your neighbors

Keeping your nose above water: surviving in an unpredictable rat race world. "Darkened so, yet shone above them all the archangel, but his face deep scars of thunder had entrenched and care sat on his faded cheek" (John Milton).

Keeps you on your toes: staying active, exercise

Kept at bay: momentarily under control

Kept on ice: going to use it when the time is right

Kick it in the ass: knocking out sluggishness

Kick the bucket, bought the farm: time to meet your maker. If one thing doesn't get you, another will.

Kick yourself in the ass: for not having done it

Kicking it: having a pleasant conversation, chewing the fat

Kill or be killed: a matter of self-defense

Kill two birds with one stone: a time-saving measure. Do two chores in about the same time frame as it would take to do one.

Killed the soldier: drinking the last drop of a bottle of whiskey

Killer instinct: keep and maintain it. "God looks upon the motive not the deed" (Unknown).

Knight in shining armor: one in a million

Knock it off: stop it

Knock on wood: do this for good luck and cross your fingers

Knock their socks off: performing superbly

Knock-them-down, drag-them-out affair: a political campaign

Knock your block off: kicking your ass, beating you up

Knocked up: pregnant. Who's your daddy? "A tenth transmitter of a foolish face" (Richard Savage).

Knocking down doors: making a great effort to accomplish it

Knocking on the door: trying to get in to participate

Knocking them dead: captivating an audience by putting them into the palm of your hand

Know it backwards and forwards: by heart, memorized

Know the score: a good idea of what is really going on

Know when to say when: you've had enough

Know where their coming from: perfectly understanding them

Know where your bread is buttered: how you support yourself. "Work without hope draws nectar in a sieve, and hope without an object cannot live" (William Wordsworth).

Know your limitations: don't get in over your head

Knowing where you stand: understanding your situation

Knowledge is power: learn as much as you can, constant and ceaseless education

Knows every trick in the book: a true professional in their chosen line of pursuit

Knows the ropes: been around, and around, and around

Knows the tricks of the trade: a prostitute

Kodak moment: one you will never forget

Labor of love: doing a worthwhile difficult task. Like writing a book, and not being "forever reading, never to be read" (Alexander Pope).

Laid an egg: a dismal performance

Land of milk and honey: paradise

Lap of luxury: pampered

Larger than life: extraordinary

Last but not least: "The last will be first" (New Testament).

Last-ditch effort: there are no alternatives left

Last fling: one final love affair

Last resort: utilizing weapons of mass destruction

Late for your own funeral: habitual tardiness

Laughing all the way to the bank: making a lot of money on a venture no one else thought possible

Law enforcement: "Who will guard the guards themselves" (Unknown).

Lay down the law: there are no ifs, ands, or buts about it, you're the person in charge

Lay of the land: found by surveying it

Lead pipe cinch: for certain

Leader of the pack: top dog

Learning the ropes: how it should be done, acquiring experience

Leave everything in the air: uncompleted

Leave it at that: don't change it

Leave it to the imagination: creativity

Leave something behind: die with favor having done your share

Leaves a bad taste in your mouth: something is just not right

Left and right: constantly

Left in the lurch: the one holding the bag, no support

Left out in the cold: abandoned, assistance from no one

Lend a helping hand: perform an errand of mercy

Less than a prayer: helpless

Lesser of two evils: Why add any more by deciding between one or the other? "Sufficient unto the day is the evil thereof" (New Testament).

Let it all hang out: lose your inhibitions

Let it go: don't do it, too risky

Let it sink in: absorption of knowledge

Let it slide: a minor insult

Let me put it this way: to communicate with precision

Let nature take its course: nature is the answer to the problems of society. "Whose works the beautiful and base contain, of vice and virtue more instructive rules, than all the sober sages of the schools" (Francis).

Let sleeping dogs lie: don't bring up old grievances, bury the hatchet. Why look for trouble? "It is nought good a sleeping dog to wake" (Geoffrey Chaucer).

Let the chips fall where they may: see what happens and take it from there

Let the dead bury the dead: keep the fire going

Let your voice be heard: acoustically gifted, eloquence

Let your work speak for itself: it's the work you do that counts, not you. "Everyone will be rewarded according to their works" (Bible).

Let's get cracking: on the move, do some work

Let's get down to business: playtime's over, get serious

Let's get it on: the final battle in the last chapter

Let's rock and roll: let's have some fun, let's get started

Letter of the law: used and abused by over zealous prosecutors

Letting go: overcoming your grief. "I am the self consumer of my woes" (John Clare).

Letting off steam: relieving stress

Letting someone off the hook: forgiving a debt

Letting your hair down: enjoying yourself

Level playing field: equal opportunity for all

License to print money: a computer whiz

License to steal: passing the bar exam

Licking your chops: close to a successful conclusion

Life goes on: millions die each year and millions are born each year, simultaneous creation and destruction

Life is fragile: handle it with prayer

Life is short: compared to what? Matter is indestructible.

Life of the mind: "Where mercy, pity, peace, and love dwell, there God dwells too" (William Blake).

Life's a bitch and then you die: things can't be all that bad

Life's little sweeteners: tobacco, booze, drugs, sex, etc.

Light my fire: excite me, turn me on

Lighten up: don't be so strict, bend and break the rules

Lightning never strikes twice in the same spot: some things only happen once. "I am as free as nature first made man, before the base laws of servitude began, when wild in the woods the noble savage ran" (John Dryden).

Like a breath of fresh air: new and exciting events

Like a broken record: saying the same thing over and over, it just won't stop

Like a candle in the wind: quickly snuffed out

Like a fish out of water: haven't the faintest clue about what they're doing, completely helpless

Like a lamb being led to slaughter: easily deceived

Like a monkey on a string: the mentality of a slave

Like an itch you can't scratch: it won't go away

Like a slap in the face: an insult

Like a snowflake in hell: doomed

Like a square peg in a round hole: you don't fit in

Like a thief in the night: a sneaky way to do it

Like a three-ring circus: confusion and disorder

Like a walk in the park: very pleasant and easy

Like being hit with a ton of bricks: caught completely unawares

Like comparing apples and oranges: trite trivial drivel

Like death warmed over: dreadful

Like father, like son: in most cases, professionals beget professionals, tradesmen beget tradesmen, and so it goes

Like it had eyes: deadly accurate

Like kicking sand in your face: trying to start a fight

Like looking for a needle in a haystack: too much time would be required to do it, if it could be done at all

Like nobody's business: a full-fledged effort

Like pulling teeth: an unpleasant task

Like spitting in the wind: a hopeless cause. "Throw sand against the wind, and the wind throws it back again" (William Blake).

Like taking candy from a baby: easily done. "To love again and again be undone" (George Byron).

Like talking to a wall: not heeding good advice. The piper piped but no one listened.

Like the pot calling the kettle black: the same fault in common

Like trying to thread a needle: a delicate job

Like watching paint dry: boring

Lion's share: the largest part, strength empowers

Lip service: "Polite meaningless words" (William Butler Yeats).

Live and learn: next time you will know better

Live and let live: try not to step on anyone's toes or rub them the wrong way. Become "more sinned against than sinning" (William Shakespeare).

Live it up: enjoy the finer things in life. "With your unconstraining voice, still persuade us to rejoice" (Wystan Hugh Auden).

Living beyond your means: spending more than you make

Living high off the hog: a luxurious lifestyle

Living on borrowed time: when it's all said and done, you have escaped death by the skin of your teeth once too often

Living on the edge: playing with fire by frequently undertaking dangerous activities

Living proof: it works, a perfect example

Living your dream: "We are such stuff as dreams are made of, and our little lives rounded by a sleep"(William Shakespeare).

Lo and behold: the beauty and the wonder of it all

Loading the dice: placing insurmountable obstacles in your way

Lock and load: fire the bullet, ask questions later

Lock, stock, and barrel: everything

Lock them up and throw away the key: child abusers, elderly abusers, and animal abusers

Locked in: a guaranteed monetary percentage rate

Locking horns: a mean argument

Long arm of the law: will reach out and grab you if you break it

Look alive: get ready, get set, go

Look back in time: to get in touch with your roots

Look before you leap: make a plan

Look the other way: it's of no concern to you, don't mention it

Look what the wind blew in: someone you haven't seen for a long time

Looking after your own: life insurance

Looking for trouble: being obnoxious

Loose lips sink ships: watch what you say. "By your words you shall be justified and by your words you will be condemned" (New Testament).

Loosen your purse strings: spend some money, if you can afford it. Keep the economy growing.

Losing steam: fatigued

Losing your cool: becoming angry

Losing your way: sidetracked, basking in your thought crime

Lost and found: evangelization

Lost at sea: bewildered

Lost in the shuffle: you can't keep track of everything

Lost your nerve: no balls left, a low testosterone level

Lost your touch: you don't have what it takes anymore

Lot of pull: influential, making offers no one can refuse

Lot of sand: guts, courage

Love and marriage: like a long boring meal with dessert served first. "Had we never loved so kindly, had we never loved so blindly, never met and never parted, we had never been broken hearted" (Robert Burns).

Love-hate relationship: the war between the sexes. He loves her, she hates him. She loves him, he hates her.

Love is blind: it knows no bounds

Love is stronger than death: it stays put in the living

Love, laughter, music, art: everything else is a pain

Love your neighbor: whoever happens to be near you at a certain time and place

Lovebirds: an over-display of affection in public

Low man on the totem pole: the last subordinate

Lower your sights: settle for something less

Lowest rung on the ladder: start here and work your way up. "Lie down where all the ladders start, in the foul rag bone shop of the heart" (William Butler Yeats).

Luck of the draw: your fate, that's the way it goes

Luck of the Irish: to be an island country. On the other hand, it's too close to England.

Made for each other: a perfect couple

Made your bones: earned respect

Make a home a home: by filling it with love

Make a killing: obtaining a fast fortune

Make a long story short: please be brief

Make a name for yourself: be all that you can be

Make a statement: concise and to the point. "And there your heart with pleasure fills, and dances with the daffodils" (William Wordsworth).

Make every day count: as something special

Make it snappy: hurry up

Make something out of nothing: change your tune

Makes your hair stand on end: very scary

Makes your head swim: a difficult problem

Make them pay: retribution

Make up your mind: decide what you want to do, set some goals

Making a big splash: a transient success

Making a clean sweep: clearing out everything impeding your progress

Making a living: earning enough money to live on

Making a move: trying to get next to a lady, hitting on her

Making a new beginning: a fresh start

Making a pig out of yourself: gluttonous gorging

Making ends meet: enough income to serve your needs

Making headway: steadily progressing

Making money hand over fist: increasing your wealth by leaps and bounds

Making someone say uncle: forcing them to give up

Making up for lost ground: doing now what should have been done before

Man does not live by bread alone: also by the sweat of his brow

Man for all seasons: well-rounded

Man's inhumanity to man: world history, a slaughter house

Marching orders: hit the road, Jack, and don't come back

Marching to the beat of a different drummer: thinking for yourself, an independent mind

Mark my words: it's going to happen

Marriage of two minds: thinking alike, on the same track

Master of your fate, captain of your soul: determine your own personal history

Match made in heaven: love at first sight. The woman doesn't nag and the man keeps his cool and chills out.

Matter of dollars and cents: if it doesn't make a profit, it can't exist. Money is a must have.

Maybe it will catch on: perhaps people will like it

Me and you against the world: you and your significant other

Me, myself, and I: sometimes you need more than this

Medical care for all: "From each according to his means, to each according to his needs" (Karl Marx and Friedrich Engels).

Menace to society: someone who cares only about one of the parts, not the whole

Method to his madness: at first sight it looks ridiculous, however, the goal is being accomplished

Mickey Mouse: cheap

Might makes right: treaties aren't worth the paper they're printed on, power enables

Mile a minute: very fast

Military bearing: correct posture

Milking it: playing it for all it's worth

Milking the system: outwitting the government

Million-dollar wound: sends you homeward bound from a combat zone

Mind over matter: the mind is superior to matter. "Fear and awe, scooped out by dreams, fall upon us when we look into our minds" (William Wordsworth).

Mind your P's and Q's: decorum

Minding the store: looking after things

Miracle of miracles: the birth of Christ, immaculate conception

Miracles never cease: "There are more things in heaven and earth than anyone has ever dreamed of in their philosophy" (William Shakespeare).

Misery loves company: to put them out of their misery

Missed the boat: lost your chance for a golden opportunity

Mixed bag: all the nationalities of the world

Mixed blessing: it's good and bad. "Port after stormy seas, sleep after heavy labor, peace after war, death after life, does surely please" (Unknown).

Mockery of justice: poor versus rich

Money is not an object: you'll pay the price no matter what the cost

Money is the root of all evil: not all evil deeds are based upon acquiring wealth

Money's tight: it's hard to come by, stick to a budget

Monkey on your back: a bad habit you can't quit, or a jinx

Monkey see, monkey do: a follower of fads

Mop it up: finish the job

More harm than good: automobiles using internal combustible engines

More power to you: the best of luck

More than one way to skin a cat: there's almost always another way to do something

More than you bargained for: not what you expected

Movers and shakers: can't get no satisfaction, power junkies

Much ado about nothing: it's not all that important

Multitasking: a computer doing several things simultaneously

Mumbo-jumbo: incoherent

My country, right or wrong: no way, Jose. Right is right, wrong is wrong. "Patriotism is the last refuge for a scoundrel" (Samuel Johnson).

My hands are tied: I can't help you

My heart aches: but I shall endure, remember, and never surrender

My lips are sealed: I won't tell anybody about it

My money's funny: I'm low on funds

Nailed to the cross: punished to the maximum, putting your head on a block

Name your weight: suggesting your own handicap in a sporting match, usually accompanied with a wager

Nature of the beast: to have problems, some more, some less

Necessity is the mother of invention: if you need something to survive, you'll do just about anything to get it

Need a fix: some substance to alter your mind and body

Need a place to stay: the homeless. "The birds have nests, the foxes dens, the son of man has no place to lay his head" (New Testament).

Need a prayer: a nearly hopeless case

Need I say anything more: was I clearly understood?

Need something to sink your teeth into: goals that may be difficult but are nevertheless worth pursuing

Need to have your head examined: seek emergency psychiatric care

Neither fish nor fowl: insufficient support

Neither here nor there: in limbo

Never a dull moment: raising a family

Never look behind: live for the moment. "For the day that is, is enough" (Eugene O'Neil).

Never say never: it just might happen

Never show your hand: keep them guessing

New lease on life: starting over with a new perspective

New money: affluent yuppies

Next time you'll know better: if there is a next time

Nice chunk of change: an ample amount of legal tender

Nice guys finish last: not all of the time

Nice touch: finesse

Night cap: a drink to end the evening

Night owl: body clock set nocturnally

Nip it in the bud: solve the problem immediately before it becomes worse

Nitpicking: making something out of nothing, fastidiously fussy

No comment: I would rather not talk about it

No contest: an unexciting sporting event

No doubt about it: you live, you love, you suffer, you die

No escape: from senility. "One must return to the childhood in their mind in order to enter into the kingdom of heaven" (New Testament).

No free lunch: you never get something for nothing. For every action there's a reaction and cause and effect.

No funny business: don't trick or deceive me

No holds barred: all's fair in love and war

No laughing matter: it's dead serious

No mean feat: way above average

No more Mister Nice Guy: from now on you're going to be as hard as nails

No news is good news: hear no evil, see no evil

No pain, no gain: pain is an indication of an injury. If it hurts, stop before it gets worse.

No place like home: it's where the heart is

No question about it: it's absolutely correct

No rest for the wicked: hell is an eternity of drudgery where no one sleeps

No rhyme or reason: it doesn't make any sense

No room for error: in some occupations, tightrope walker, iron worker, brain surgeon, that sort of thing

No room to talk: you're not any better, maybe worse

No shit, Sherlock: everyone knows that, it ain't nothing new

No sirree, Bob: absolutely not

No skin off my nose: it matters little to me, I could care less

No spring chicken: getting up in years

No strings attached: there are no preexisting conditions binding you to it

No sweat off my back: suit yourself

No turning back: when you reach a certain point

No two ways about it: to learn a language you must memorize it

Nobody put a gun to your head: not forced to do it

Not a care in the world: children

Not all it's cracked up to be: the electronic revolution

Not by a long shot: I won't do it

Not following the crowd: going your own way. Be a leader, not a follower.

Not for anything in the world: I will never do that

Not for the life of me: I can't figure it out

Not getting any younger: you can't do some things you used to be able to do. "My best years may be gone but I wouldn't want them back, not with the fire in me now" (Samuel Beckett).

Not going there: I won't discuss that

Nothing in life comes easy: except for having your heart broke

Nothing is constant: but change. "You must lose your life in order to gain it" (New Testament).

Nothing to sneeze at: a considerable amount

Nothing to write home about: a mediocre occurrence at best

Not in this life: infinite eternal happiness. "She said less sad of speech than mild, all this is when he comes, her eyes prayed and she smiled" (Unknown).

Not long for this world: a reckless person, baiting the law of averages

Not made out of money: just getting by

Not on the up and up: illegitimate

Not on your life: never ever

Not playing with a full deck: off your rocker, mentally challenged, a few quarts low

Not the end of the world: it's really not all that bad, you'll get over it

Not the marrying kind: a confirmed bachelor

Not to worry: I'll take care of it

Not up to it: don't feel like doing it

Now and then: occasionally

Nowhere to turn: stuck in the middle

Now I've seen everything: excuse me, no way

Now you're cooking: on a winning streak, doing your best

Of its own accord: history repeats itself

Off the beaten track: hard to find, remote

Off the top of your head: the best you can remember right now

Off the wall: spontaneous and unclear

Off to the races: nothing can stop you

Old before your time: not adhering to the law of moderation, overindulgence

Old money: inheriting it to and fro, generation to generation, don't have to work

Old wives' tale: it was never true, but is repeatedly told time and again

On a bender: an alcoholic binge

On again, off again: sometimes it works, sometimes it doesn't work

On a higher plane: way above the rest

On a roll: good things are happening in consecutive order

On a scale of one to ten: ten is the best, one is the worst. Two through nine vary relatively.

On Cloud Nine: a happy camper

On easy street: good health and enough money to live a life of luxury in a tropical climate

On my list: for retaliation

On pins and needles: excitedly anxious about an event soon to happen

On the bubble: the last one out of the money in a poker tournament. "The unkindest cut of all" (William Shakespeare).

On the chopping block: marked for elimination

On the double: do it quickly

On the edge of your seat: intense suspense

On the fence: undecided

On the fly: happenstance

On the hot seat: accused

On the lam: a fugitive from justice

On the make: hoping to be picked up

On the outside looking in: observing but not willing or able to participate

On the run: a wanted person by the law

On the same page: in complete agreement

On the sidelines: waiting to participate if needed

On the stump: giving a speech

On the up and up: doing it right straight from the heart

On the wagon: presently a teetotaler

On your best behavior: to make a good impression

On your high horse: bragging

On your last legs: in very poor health

On your nickel: paying for all the expenses

On your own: self-reliant, no support

On your watch: the responsibility rests on your shoulders

Once bitten, twice shy: wary of a harmful past event repeating itself

Once in a blue moon: it seldom, if ever, happens

Once upon a time: it was, it will be

Once you start you can't stop: an addictive pleasure

One after the other: sequential

One and the same: but labeled with different names

One day you're up, the next day you're down: mood swings

One drink too many: over the limit

One foot in the grave: close to death. "Like snow that falls upon a river, a moment white, then gone forever" (Robert Burns).

One for all, all for one: the human race as it should be. "With compassion for all and malice towards none" (Abraham Lincoln).

One for the road: a last drink before leaving a bar and going home

One hand washes the other: tit for tat, quid pro quo, do me a good turn and I'll return the favor

One last shot: a final attempt

One man's trash is another man's treasure: how eBay began and flourishes

One shot deal: it won't happen again

One step away: from who knows what

One step forward, two steps back: like the myth of Sisyphus, your effort is accomplishing nothing

One step too far: overreaching

One that got away: you can't win them all

One thing led to another: the theory of evolution by natural selection. Darwinism. "Man still bears in his bodily frame the indelible stamp of his lowly origin" (Charles Darwin).

One too many: Bible thumpers

One way of looking at it: a place where time does not exist

One way or another: everyone pays and everyone owes

Only the good die young: they did not have enough time to become really bad. "Each soul is the hostage of its deeds" (Koran).

Only the strong survive: how long?

Open-and-shut case: the facts are indisputable no matter how you look at it. "What is hateful to yourself, do not do to your fellow man" (Talmud).

Opened a can of worms: there's a lot more to it than you first thought

Open for business: ready to go

Open mind: not set in your thinking

Open to interpretation: different opinions on a subject

Operating on different wavelengths: poor communication

Opposites of the same coin: too much to do, too little to do

Organized crime: dysfunctional dissidents, unwise guys

Our days are numbered: how many? What's the number?

Our paths may cross again: we might meet again in the future

Out for the count: immobilized

Out like a light: sound asleep

Out of sight: extraordinarily excellent

Out of sight, out of mind: absence doesn't make the heart grow fonder

Out of the clear blue sky: you never saw it coming

Out of thin air: suddenly appearing

Out of this world: really great, absolutely awesome

Out of your element: disinclined

Out of your league: too good for you, overmatched

Out of your mind: not with it

Out with the old, in with the new: each succeeding generation reaps the benefits and detriments of the previous ones. "My thoughts are with the dead, with them I live in long past years" (Walter Landor).

Over my dead body: if I can stop it, no way it's going to happen

Over the hill: way past your prime

Over the top: unrealistic, larger than life

Pack it in: it's useless to continue

Packed to the gills: a full house, standing room only

Packs a punch: a contender

Pact with the devil: not recommended, it might steal your soul

Paid your dues: you've done your share

Pain in the ass: a troublesome thing entirely

Paint the town red: cause for celebration

Painting a picture: clarification

Pales in comparison: not nearly as good

Parting is such sweet sorrow: "Today will die tomorrow, time stoops to no one's lure" (Charles Swinburne).

Parting of ways: complete disagreement over a serious matter, irreconcilability

Pass it along: tell people about it

Pass it around: sharing. "It's better to give than to receive" (New Testament).

Passing the buck: an artful dodger

Past, present, and future: today becomes the past, when tomorrow the future is cast. Time will never cease, the present is always deceased.

Past your bedtime: it's time to go to sleep

Path of least resistance: the road too many take

Patting yourself on the back: self-aggrandizement

Paving the way: opening a new frontier

Paying your debt to society: pledge your allegiance. "Suit the action to the word" (William Shakespeare).

Peace beyond understanding: when the iceman cometh

Peace of mind: living in harmony with nature. "Now every field, now every tree is green, now nature's fairest face is seen" (William Wordsworth).

Penned in: a feeling of confinement

Penny, penny, penny: chintzy

Penny wise and pound foolish: competent with small matters but anything greater is over your head

Perish the thought: I hope it will never happen

Phantoms of delight: breathtakingly beautiful women

Phone's ringing off the wall: too many calls or none at all

Pick and choose: take only the best, the pick of the litter

Pick up some ground: to stay in the game

Pick up the pieces: start all over again

Picking Pikipski: playing with your toenails

Picking up steam: acceleration

Picking your name out of a hat: randomness

Picture perfect: photographs reveal every detail

Pie in the sky: unrealistic, only in your dreams

Piece of ass: getting laid, got lucky

Pieces of a soul: letters

Pillars of society: the greatest of great hypocrites

Pinching pennies: on a very tight budget

Pipe dream: fantasizing

Pit of your stomach: uncanny feelings here set off an alarm

Pitch a bitch: complain, moan and groan about it

Places to go and things to do: passing time

Play all the angles: determine every possible way of winning

Play ball: cooperate, be a team player

Play by the book: follow the rules

Play it as it lies: you have no choices in the matter. "Thou hast nor youth nor age, but as it were, an after dinner's sleep dreaming of both" (William Shakespeare).

Play it to the hilt: for all it's worth

Play the percentages: calculate the odds

Play to the bitter end: never give in, don't lose heart

Play your cards right: be a force to be reckoned with

Playing both ends against the middle: deceiving your partners in a business to gain control of it

Playing both sides of the fence: USA foreign policy

Playing dumb: pretending not to know what happened

Playing favorites: unfairly choosing one over the other

Playing for all the marbles: your entire bankroll is at stake

Playing for keeps: dead serious

Playing hardball: getting down to business

Playing hard to get: if you have the goods

Playing into their hands: doing exactly what they want you to do

Playing mind games: deliberately misleading

Playing musical chairs: going around in circles

Playing right into your hands: just what you want them to do

Playing second fiddle: subordinate

Playing tag: unable to contact one another

Playing the field: available for love

Plug the holes: prevent possible mishaps

Pocket change: a nuisance

Pocket pair: two cards of the same denomination dealt to you in Texas Hold'em

Poetic justice: a higher power setting things right, divine intervention

Poetry in motion: a series of graceful movements

Pointing the finger: an accusation

Politically correct: speaking euphemistically

Pomp and circumstance: a royal array

Popped into your head: suddenly recalled. "Memory is the diary we all keep" (Oscar Wilde).

Pops up anywhere: Lady Luck

Possession is nine-tenths of the law: if you have possession of something, you probably own it

Pounding the pavement: looking for work

Poverty in America: where the Melting Pot lives, and they melt in summer when tempers fly

Practice makes perfect: doing something over and over again should make you proficient at it. There's no substitute for practice.

Practice what you preach: set a good example, keep your word as a code of conduct

Prepare the way for others: become a pioneer

Preserve the memory: write it down

Pressure cooker: gravity bearing down on us

Pro and con: some for, some against. Some good, some bad.

Problem drinker: you can't get enough of it

Product of your environment: where and how a person is raised, in a large degree, determines their future. "That we may trace the lineaments of a plummet measured face" (William Butler Yeats).

Pull no punches: do it with all your might, don't hold back

Pull your own weight: do your share of the work

Pull yourself together: snap out of it

Pulled a disappearing act: avoiding you

Pulled a fast one: a slick swindle. "Like a guilty thing upon a fearful summons" (William Shakespeare).

Pulled it off: beating the odds

Pulled the plug: bringing it abruptly to a halt. "From you my labors wait their last reward" (Bible).

Pulled the strings: the real culprit of a crime

Pulled your pocket: running a background check

Pulling out all the stops: doing everything possible to complete it

Pulling strings: using favoritism or bribery to affect the outcome

Pulling the wool over your eyes: a con artist trying to con you

Punch palaces: saloons where brawls frequently occur

Punching their lights out: inflicting a severe beating, making them wish they were never born

Pure as the driven snow: a virgin

Push the button: get it started

Pushed to the edge: having bad luck and close to a nervous breakdown. "They are times that try your soul" (Thomas Paine).

Pushing up daisies: your final resting place

Put a ceiling on it: limit the number

Put all your cards on the table: sometimes it's beneficial to do this when negotiating a business deal

Put all your rotten eggs into one basket: so you can keep track of them

Put a new spin on it: do it completely different

Put a price on their head: encouraging bounty hunters

Put a sock in it: shut up, zip up your lip

Put in an appearance: to show you still exist

Put it in the vault: keep it between you and me

Put it in writing: if a dispute arises, you have proof of your part of the bargain

Put it on ice: do it later

Put it on the back burner: it's more practical to do it at a later date

Put it to rest: for heaven's sake, finish it!

Put on hold: it's taking longer than expected

Put on the hot seat: forced to come up with some answers

Put on your best face: friendly and laidback

Put that in your pipe and smoke it: gloating with triumphant glee

Put the icing on the cake: make a sweet deal sweeter

Put their head on a platter: maximum retribution

Put them in their place: right where they belong

Put them on the map: by becoming famous or infamous

Put the pedal to the metal: go all out, full blast

Put the squeeze on: make them pay up

Put through the mill: a grueling experience

Put your best foot forward: don't backslide

Put your mind to it: make it work

Put your money where your mouth is: put up or shut up. "Pity would be no more, if we did not make somebody poor" (William Blake).

Put your pants on one leg at a time: humble and modest, not on a pedestal

Put yourself in my shoes: experience vicariously what I have been through

Put yourself in their place: capital punishment applied to a person not guilty of the crime. "If you do it to the least of my brethren, you do it also to me" (New Testament).

Put your two cents in: speak up

Putting on airs: look how great I am

Putting the arm on you: a favor seeker

Putting the pieces together: figuring out the puzzle by doing this in the proper sequence

Putting two and two together: "The Creator made all living things in pairs" (Koran).

Putting words in your mouth: saying you said what you never said

Putting you on: playing a practical joke

Putting your affairs in order: do this when you have a terminal illness, and when a judge sentences you to a long term in prison

Putting your foot down: adamant

Putting your house in order: doing what must be done

Putty in their hands: when a man loves a woman, vice versa, and same, same

Question mark: success or failure

Quit while the quitting is good: desist before it brings you down

R

Rabbit's foot: any good luck charm

Racing the clock: warding off the effects of aging or disease

Rags: a starting poker hand in the lowest probability of winning category

Rags to riches: a sudden windfall

Raining cats and dogs: a heavy downpour

Raked over the coals: an excruciating ordeal

Rap sheet: recorded criminal history

Rattling your cage: a blatant attempt to upset you

Reach for the stars: don't place limitations on yourself. "Was Christ a man like us? Ah! Let us try if we, then, too, can be such men as he" (Matthew Arnold).

Read between the lines: try to come close to the truth

Read my lips: I mean what I'm saying

Read the fine print: to determine how badly you're getting screwed

Read them the riot act: set your terms in stone

Ready to explode: pushed to the limit

Ready to let them have it: a good tongue thrashing

Ready to march down the aisle: a desire to get hitched

Ready to meet your maker: content

Ready to pounce: on the hunt

Ready to roll the dice: the offer wasn't good enough, prepare to take a chance on getting something better

Ready to take the plunge: wanting to get married

Ready, willing, and able: time to compete

Red carpet treatment: hospitality at its best. "Be bright and jovial among your guests" (William Shakespeare).

Red tape: bureaucratic rigmarole

Reduced to this: unhappy with your present pitiful condition

Rekindle it: a former love affair

Rest assured: God's in heaven and all is right with the universe

Rest on your laurels: take a permanent break, retire

Riding on their coattails: fawning obsequious bootlickers

Riding the wave of popularity: staying with it until it subsides

Right at your fingertips: within reach

Right back where you started from: this is where we all end up at, if we last that long. Senility is childhood begun anew.

Right down to the wire: a close race, too close to call

Right-hand man: loyal and trustworthy

Right off the bat: from the very beginning

Right on the money: just how you want it to be, perfect

Right up your alley: it suits you just fine

Ring around the rosie: where you're going nobody knows

Rings a bell: a vague recollection

Rise among the pack: become top dog

Rise and shine: get your lazy butt out of bed. Up and at 'em.

Rite of passage: sifting through the sieve. "What doesn't kill you makes you stronger" (Friedrich Nietzsche).

Robbing the cradle: an older person having an affair with someone much younger than them

Rock solid: dependable, you can count on it

Rocked the world: a major historical event

Roll with the punches: if you're knocked down, get back up. "Made weak by time and fate, but still strong in will to strive, to seek, to find, and not to yield" (Alfred Tennyson).

Rolled-up trips: a poker hand that begins with three of a kind in Seven-Card Stud

Rolling along: smooth sailing

Rome wasn't built in a day: some things take a long time to accomplish, brick by brick

Roped into something: bound to a long-term commitment you're not especially pleased with

Rotten to the core: cursed from birth

Rough around the edges: irritated

Rub their noses in it: the way it really is, reality

Rubbing elbows: socializing

Rubbing it in: overly critical

Rubbing someone the wrong way: insulting them intentionally or unintentionally

Ruffled a few feathers: causing quit a stir

Rule of thumb: standard practice

Rules of society: manacles forged by minds

Rumor has it: bullshit abounds

Rumors are rife: inconclusive rampant gossip

Run a tab: your credit is good

Run for cover: protect yourself

Runs in the family: the gene pool

Runs the show: the boss

Running away from the pack: leading by a wide margin

Running away with it: an insurmountable lead

Running like a top: a machine in perfect working order

Running scared: hiding from a challenge

Running with the pack: joining the crowd

Running your mouth: speaking nonsense

Sad but true: saying one thing but doing another. "Fooled by hope they favor the deceit" (John Dryden).

Salt of the Earth: hardworking honest people

Same old, same old: redundancy

Sand bagging: concealing your true strength

Saps your energy: it takes too much out of you

Save it for a rainy day: funds held in reserve in case of an emergency

Save the day: stand up and be counted

Save your soul: "Love God with all your heart, mind, body, and soul. And love your neighbor as yourself" (New Testament).

Say it ain't so: tell me it's a lie

Scared to death: "We all owe God a debt of death, pay it today and you won't owe it tomorrow" (William Shakespeare).

School of hard knocks: growing up on the wrong side of the tracks and learning your lessons the hard way. "In a world more full of weeping than you can understand" (William Butler Yeats).

Scout's honor: honest to God

Scraping the bottom of the barrel: willing to accept less than you hoped for

Scratching your head: puzzled

Screwed blue and tattooed: there's no way out

Seasons come and seasons go: "If winter comes, can spring be far behind" (Percy Shelly).

Second guessing: annoyingly saying it was wrong and should have been done another way

Second wind: reinvigorated, ready to go again

See how the other half lives: the same as you do. "Our bodies feel, wherever they be, against or with our will" (William Wordsworth).

Seeing double: sober up

Seeing eye to eye: absolute agreement

Seeing the bigger picture: using your imagination to forecast what may occur sometime in the future

Seeing the light: living with dignity

Seeing the light at the end of the tunnel: a difficult job is nearly completed

Seeing the writing on the wall: knowing what's about to happen because of the way things are transpiring

Seen the light of day: discovered who, what, why, and where you are

Sending a message: terrorists

Sense of direction: a built in compass, navigator

Sense of humor: knowing when to laugh and what to laugh at

Sense of the greater good: serving your country. The individual dies, the nation lives on.

Sent through a loop: going over something repeatedly to make sense of it

Separate the men from the boys: when the going gets tough, the tough get going, the boys quit

Service with a smile: fast food facade

Set for life: follow the Ten Commandments. "The sum of all ten is, you should love more than others, God above" (Clough).

Set the record straight: clear up any mistakes

Setting the bar too high: your goal is impossible, settle for less

Setting the world on fire: astound everyone with your talent and ability

Setting up shop: starting a business

Setting your sights higher: ambition, go for it

Shadow of your former self: "What the hell happened?" (Steve McQueen)

Shake a leg: get moving

Shake their tails: women do this to attract men

Shame on you: behaving badly

Shape up or ship out: change your act or get dumped

Share and share alike: all the natural resources. "That men may rise on stepping stones of their dead selves to higher things" (Georg Goethe).

She swears like a sailor: a woman whose speech is packed with obscenities, a mouth like a truck driver

Shed some more light on the subject: clarify it

Ships passing in the night: meeting someone for the first time and never seeing or hearing from them again

Shit can it: throw it away

Shit-faced: inebriated, wasted

Shit happens: unexpected catastrophic turning of events

Shit or get off the pot: do something

Shoot: tell me what's on your mind

Shoot and ask questions later: before it's too late, let God sort them out

Shooting fish in a barrel: too easy

Shortest route to an early grave: staying sober and hard work

Shot yourself in the foot: causing your own downfall. "The fault lies not in our stars but in ourselves" (William Shakespeare).

Should of, could of, would of: but did not

Shoving it down your throat: propaganda

Show your true colors: be true to yourself. "Join yourself with the universe and make all things fit as one with that all" (John Donne).

Showing you the ropes: teaching a newcomer

Shrugging your shoulders: nonchalant

Shuffle off to Buffalo: take a trip

Sick and tired of it: you can't stand it anymore

Sick puppy: mentally deranged, psychopathic

Sight for sore eyes: exclaim this when you see a friend you haven't seen for quite awhile

Sign of the times: the events in the news reflect the kind of society and world we live in

Signed, sealed, and delivered: closure

Silence is golden: meditating in solitude away from the multitude. "There to find a life within itself, to breathe without mankind" (George Byron).

Silencing the critics: improving immensely

Simply stated: the crux of good speech and writing

Sit on it: don't do anything yet

Sit tight: wait

Sitting on top of the world: having all that your heart desires

Sitting pretty: financially secure

Six of one, half dozen of the other: the same thing. Like politicians, who uniformly drink from the taxpayers' trough.

Six ways to Sunday: every possibility

Sixth sense: indescribable

Sizing them up: acute observation

Sky's the limit: let your imagination run wild

Slave driver: forcing people under your authority to work too hard

Sleep on it: take some time to think it over

Slept like a baby: an uninterrupted sound sleep. "Can sleep be death when life is but a dream" (William Blake).

Slipping between the cracks: succumbing to temptations of pleasure by making them your only pursuit

Slowly but surely: you reach old age, if you live that long

Smacked upside your head: some people need a good ass whipping

Smooth it over: make amends

Snail mail: delivered by a human being into a box attached on or near a home

Snap out of it: stop daydreaming

Snug as a bug in a rug: comfortable

So far, so good: you've made it through another day. "The night is long that never finds the day" (William Shakespeare).

So much for that: an unsuccessful attempt

So near, yet so far: conquering yourself. "The absolute spirit's quest for and conquest of its own self" (Georg Hegel).

So to speak: that's one way of saying it

Soak it all in: acquire the knowledge of the subject

Soften the blow: lessen the shock of the bad news

Soften them up: friendly persuasion

Sold down the river: cheating you out of your fair share by giving you the short end of the stick

Some big shoes to fill: taking charge of something from someone who did great work, a tough row to hoe

Some people: rudeness

Some people never learn: repeatedly making the same mistakes

Somebody's got to do it: a dirty but necessary job

Someone giving you the cold shoulder: formerly friendly but now they act like they hardly know you

Something always goes wrong: "Even the best laid plans often go awry" (William Shakespeare).

Something came up: an unforeseeable event

Something or nothing: you win what someone loses or you lose what someone wins, it's all the same in the end

Something to chew on: food for thought

Something to tide you over: a short-term loan

Something's got to give: one way or another

Sometimes the truth is hard to swallow: "A prophet is without honor in his own country" (New Testament).

Sometimes you only get one shot: take it

Son of man: sower of fine seed, the saved

Song and dance: excuse upon excuse upon excuse

Sore loser: who isn't, but be a good sport

Sounds like a personal problem: keep it to yourself

Sounds too good to be true: then it's probably not true

Source of wonder: the gift of beauty. Beauty is drawn to beauty.

Sowed your wild oats: you're now a grown-up person. "When you're a child, you act like a child, but when you become an adult, put away childish things and act like an adult" (Bible).

Spark that ignites it: whatever inspired you, and then the creative juices started to flow

Speak of the devil: arriving, when just prior to your arrival, you were the topic of conversation

Speak with a forked tongue: lying

Speaking out of turn: butting in on a conversation

Speaks for itself: self-evident

Spilled the beans: disclosing a secret

Spinning a yarn: telling a tale

Spoken too soon: then it happened or didn't happen

Square off: fight it out

Stacking the deck: dishonesty

Stakes are too high: your bankroll can't take the risk

Staking a claim: forcibly asserting ownership

Stand your ground: don't be a wussy and run away

Standing out in a crowd: unlike everyone else

Stands the test of time: the New Gospel

Stand-up guy: takes a stand when the situation warrants it, regardless of the consequences

Staring down the barrel of a gun: "Fear not that which can kill the body. Fear only that which can kill the soul" (New Testament).

Start at the bottom: then work your way up

Start at the top: and stay there

Started to snowball: rapidly becoming larger

Starting to sink in: beginning to understand it

Starve a cold, feed a fever: you tell me and then we'll both know

State of grace: having God on your side

State of mind: staying calm and fearless come what may. "Meet with triumph and disaster, and treat these two imposters just the same" (Rudyard Kipling).

Stay in touch: contact family and friends occasionally

Stay put: don't go anywhere

Stay the course: don't waver

Steady the ladder: assist someone who needs help

Steamers: poker players trying to recover from a "bad beat" by raising and re-raising with almost any hand, also known as "on a tilt"

Step by step: the job gets done

Step outside: let's settle it once and for all

Step up to the plate: answer the call

Stepping out of line: misbehaving

Stick it out: until your time comes

Stick to the game plan: don't deviate

Stick to your guns: unshakably defiant

Stick with it: when the going is good

Stick with the basics: don't complicate matters

Sticking your head into the sand: you want to hide but it's impossible

Sticks in the craw: it doesn't seem right

Sticks out like a sore thumb: notably conspicuous

Sticky fingers: dipping into the till

Stiff as a board: drunk as a skunk

Still have some lead left in your pencil: an older sexually functioning male

Still in the hunt: success remains possible

Still kicking: alive and well

Still standing: after all these years

Still wet behind the ears: an apprentice without any experience

Stirred up a hornet's nest: the USA invasion of Iraq

Stitch in time saves nine: perform a job when it needs to be done or it will become more difficult to complete

Stock and trade: how you carry yourself. "The content of your character" (Martin Luther King).

Stomping grounds: where you grew up

Stop and think twice: before making a commitment

Stop, look, and listen: sharpen your senses

Stopping traffic: an extremely attractive woman, a stunner

Straight as an arrow: attracted solely to the opposite sex

Straighten up and fly right: discard all your bad habits and walk the straight and narrow road. "All spirits are enslaved which serve things evil" (Percy Shelly).

Strange bedfellows: perpetual antagonists in agreement

Stranger in a strange land: not feeling at home, homesick

Stretch runner: full throttle near the finish line

Stretch your legs: go for a walk

Stretched too thin: insufficient assets

Strike a chord: drawing forth emotions through a work of art

Strike while the iron is hot: do it while the opportunity is ripe

Stuck between a rock and a hard place: a complete dilemma. No matter what you do, you cannot improve your predicament.

Stuck in the middle: can't take sides

Stunts your growth: indolence

Suffer the consequences: of all of your actions

Suit yourself: do what you want, I don't care

Sunday driver: an overly cautious automobile operator

Supply and demand: everyone gets what they want by selling and buying. "Getting and spending we lay waste our powers, little we see in nature is ours" (William Wordsworth).

Swallowed it hook, line, and sinker: falling for a joke

Swallowing insults: sticks and stones will break my bones, but names will never hurt me

Swept under the carpet: getting away with it by knowing people in high places with clout

Swinging after the bell: unsportsmanlike conduct

Swings both ways: ambidextrous

Switching gears: going from one topic to another

Take a deep breath: pause and contemplate

Take a good look in the mirror: for a thorough self-examination

Take a hike: leave the premises immediately

Take a hint: you're not welcome here

Take a load off: sit down and relax, make yourself comfortable

Take a powder: go away

Take a rain check: postpone it

Take a slow boat to China: get out of my sight and stay out

Take a stab at it: give it a quick try

Take care of your equipment: and it will take care of you

Take hold of yourself: get a grip on things. "Deep distress can humanize the soul" (William Wordsworth).

Take it all in stride: the bumps and the bruises

Take it like a man: don't be a cry baby when the "slings and arrows of outrageous fortune" (William Shakespeare) pass your way

Take it one day at a time: don't rush headlong into it. "Patience is a virtue" (Unknown).

Take it or leave it: the opportunity to escape eternal damnation. Be saved, not damned.

Take it outside: the argument between yourselves

Take it to the heart: store the treasure there

Take me in: begging for shelter

Take my word for it: sincerity

Take off the gloves: wipe them off the face of the Earth. Search and destroy them.

Take on all comers: when you're at the top of your game

Take the money and run: quit while you're ahead

Take your hat off: offer congratulations

Taken for a ride: cheated out of something

Taken to the cleaners: gambling emptied your pockets

Takes its toll: vice after vice, but oh so nice, like sugar and spice

Takes the edge off: recreational activities

Takes your breath away: rapture

Taking a beating: no luck at all

Taking a dump: moving your bowels

Taking all day and night: a snail's pace

Taking it easy: relaxing

Taking it on the chin: absorbing punishment

Taking someone under your wing: looking out for a person who is much younger and less experienced than you

Taking something for granted: at any time and place it can be taken away

Taking the law into your own hands: thinking you're above the law

Talk is cheap: performing good deeds, not just talking about them, are the most valuable of valuable things. "Whatever you give shall rebound to your advantage" (Koran).

Talk of the town: the latest local scandal

Talk to me: what on earth is troubling you?

Talking behind your back: snip, snip, snipity-snip

Talking out of both sides of your mouth: not making any sense

Talking up a storm: loquaciousness

Talking your ear off: you can't get a word in edgewise

Tap a kidney: relieve yourself, take a leak

Tax shelters: legalized theft

Teach someone a lesson: using a harsh admonition in the hope they will mend their ways

Telegraphing: showing your hand without knowing it

Tell it like it is: tell no lies. "Thought and language are instruments of an art" (Oscar Wilde).

Tell me about it: reminding someone about something they would rather forget

Tender is the night: alone with your sweetheart

Test of wills: staying power prevails

Testing the waters: experimenting and seeing where it takes you

Textbook: just right

Thanks but no thanks: I don't want it

That hit the spot: a refreshing drink, pause for the cause

That pill is hard to swallow: I don't believe you, try to convince me otherwise

That's a given: widely known

That's all she wrote: it's over and done with

That's all there is to it: simplicity

That's a thought: very interesting, I'll keep it in mind

That's for me to know and for you to find out: discover it on your own

That's highway robbery: an overpriced commodity

That's how the cookie crumbles: there's nothing you can do about it

That's life: woe is me

That's neither here nor there: it has no bearing on the subject

That's not my cup of tea: I don't like it

That's par for the course: the average way to do it

That's that: story over

That's the beauty of it: anyone can understand it

That's the last straw: you will tolerate it no longer

That's the most: amazingly awesome

That's the oldest trick in the book: an overused contrivance

That's the ticket: the best way to do it

That's the way it goes: you can't change it. "For wit and judgment are ever at strife" (Alexander Pope).

That's the way the ball bounces: fate and destiny combined

That's what I'm talking about: expressing incredible joy

That's what it's all about: caring about and for each other, love one another

The apple doesn't fall far from the tree: nepotism. The family that connives together, sticks together. Blood is thicker than water.

The beginning of the end: when you reach old age. "Divorces are made in heaven" (Oscar Wilde).

The best things in life are free: there are some things that money can't buy

The Big Bang: creation of an enterprise for profit

The bigger they are the harder they fall: think about this when defending yourself against a big bully

The blind leading the blind: the unable following the incompetent

The bottom fell out: a sudden drastic reversal of fortune

The buck stops here: the person in charge will handle the problem

The bum's rush: getting rid of someone surreptitiously

The coast is clear: it's safe to proceed

The complete picture: everything involving the topic

The cornerstone of civilization: survival of the fittest

The cream always rises to the top: the best in their profession or sport almost always emerge at or near the top spot

The cure for what ails you: drinking an alcoholic beverage for medicinal purposes

The cutting edge: the latest innovation

The dating game: wine and dine, sweet talk, and taking your time

The devil may care: a carefree attitude

The die is cast: there's no way to stop it

The door swings both ways: opposite viewpoints

The easy way out: suicide or self-murder. "The Lord gives and the Lord takes away" (Bible).

The end justifies the means: accomplishing it no matter what the cost

The end of the line: it doesn't go any further. "Everyone dies but no one is dead" (Budda).

The facts of life: sometimes you get the bear, sometimes the bear gets you

The far side: an unknown dimension

The final answer: Apocalypse soon. "That God, which ever lives and loves, one God, one law, one element, to which the whole creation moves" (Alfred Tennyson).

The four corners of the world: east, west, north, and south rounded off

The game is up: the con is caught

The golden years: growing old is not for sissies

The good old college try: giving all that you got

The good old days: gone but not forgotten

The grass is always greener on the other side: the afterlife is better than the present life, for some of us

The great wheel of destiny: eternally moved by love

The inside circle: a higher echelon clique

The jig is up: your nefarious scheme has been detected

The joint is jumping: a crowded bar where everyone is having a good time

The key ingredient: makes the ordinary extraordinary

The last hurrah: undertaking one final adventure

The last walk: a condemned person's path to their execution

The Lord knows why: the way it is. "Some natural sorrow, loss, or pain, that has been, and may be again" (William Wordsworth).

The man on the street: an average Joe

The man with the plan: God. "Expatiate freely over this scene of man, a mighty maze, but not without a plan" (Alexander Pope).

The meaning of life: taking it on one day at a time. "Each day is a daring adventure or nothing" (Helen Keller).

The means at your disposal: use what's readily available

The missing link: question mark sublime

The more the merrier: having more than one of a good thing is merry indeed

The more things change, the more they stay the same: our outward appearance changes, but inside the spirit remains the same. "I heard the old, old men say, everything alters, and one by one we drop away" (William Butler Yeats).

The name of the game: "Life must be seen before it can be known" (Unknown).

The natives are restless: a riot may be brewing

The natural order of things: compassion over brutality. "The modest and merciful shall inherit the Earth" (New Testament).

The nose knows: instincts on full alert

The nuts: an unbeatable poker hand

The one that got away: had it, then lost it

The only language they understand: force

The other side of the coin: the opposite of something, like darkness and light

The outcome was uncertain: you will never know

The pause that refreshes: a cold drink on a hot day

The pen is mightier than the sword: a walk through a large library proves this

The Periodic Table of the Elements: all of everything

The pickings are slim: there's not much remaining of any value

The price of power: becoming a target for lunatics and soldiers under authority

The proof is in the pudding: how it ultimately comes out will determine one's opinion of it

The pursuit of happiness: an even break

The race against the clock: doing whatever you can to slow the aging process down

The razor's edge: one slip and it's all over

The real thing: authenticity

The rich get richer and the poor get poorer: those who have the means depriving those who have the needs. "The profit of the earth is for all" (Bible).

The right stuff: all the makings

The rites of spring: a rebirth of life

The road to hell is paved with good intentions: "The gates of Hell are open night and day, smooth the descent and easy is the way. But, to return and view the cheerful skies, in this the task and mighty labor lies" (John Dryden).

The roof fell in: bankrupt, sunk but salvageable

The runaround: constant evasion

The second time around: a previous love affair begun anew

The sheer force of your character: shows who you are and what you stand for

The shoe's on the other foot: present-day South Africa

The show must go on: when tragedy strikes, it's best to stay busy and let time cure the wound

The social order: inheritance sustains it, revolution will destroy it

The sticks: rural areas

The story of my life: this, that, and the other things

The straw that broke the camel's back: one mistake too many leads to disaster

The sweet by and by: heavenly paradise

The thrill is gone: you've done it too many times

The tide is turning: a good omen

The tide will turn: you'll get your chance, be patient

The time and place: of your own choosing

The time of your life: unsurpassed enjoyment. Also keep in mind, every second counts.

The truth will be revealed: at some moment in time

The turning point: the worst part is over

The ultimate sacrifice: dying for a good cause

The whole ball of wax: all the facts and items pertaining to the matter, the whole nine yards

The whole kit and caboodle: all of it

The whole package: a person with character and presence. "From the first you were, in the end you are" (Charles Swinburne).

There ain't no justice: not here but hereafter

There are exceptions to every rule: nothing is absolute

There are two laws: one for the rich and one for the poor

There but through the grace of God go I: you've committed the same reprehensible act but were not caught

There goes the neighborhood: another freeway, airport expansion, or shopping mall

There's a lot of unanswered questions: you got that right

There's always a dark cloud over the horizon: something bad is bound to happen, share your grief with someone. "In vain in secrecy we assuage our cares, concealed they gather tenfold rage" (Lewis).

There's a pot of gold at the end of every rainbow: applying yourself diligently to the job of making a living should earn you enough money to meet your needs

There's hope for all of us: "Ask and you shall receive" (New Testament).

There's hope on the horizon: things are starting to look up

There's more to life than this: the same thing over and over

There's more to this than meets the eye: the microscopic and macroscopic entities are both infinite. "Of what is past, passing, or to come" (William Butler Yeats).

There's only one way out: try to find it. "Life is but a sport and a diversion" (Koran).

These are spoken for: hands off

They act like they own the place: an employee or guest going beyond the bounds of decorum

They come and they go: the good times, the bad times. "And this too shall pass" (Unknown).

They don't build them like they used to: craftsmanship in prior times was much better than it is in present times

They don't go as far as they used to: dollars

They like to kick you when you're down: mean-spirited people. "For arrogance and hatred are the wares peddled in the thoroughfares" (William Butler Yeats).

They never knew what hit them: a deadly surprise

They saw you coming: a lamb ready for fleecing

They shoot horses, don't they: euthanasia

They won't budge: recalcitrant

They'll hound you to death: the news media. Princess Diana, Sam Sheppard, and on and on.

They'll suck you in: if you're a sucker

Things are looking up: bright prospects

Think fast: catch it, quick reflexes

Think money grows on trees: spendthrifts

Think their shit doesn't stink: snobs

Think they're special: can cut in line

Thin-skinned: easily offended

Third time's a charm: perhaps

This animal is vicious if attacked: the first law of self-defense and self-preservation

This is it for me: I'm folding up my tent, it's senseless to continue

Thousand-yard stare: post-traumatic stress

Three-dog night: the weather is so cold you need three dogs in bed with you to keep you warm

Three hots and a cot: room and board in prison

Three sheets to the wind: intoxicated

Three-time loser: impossible to rehabilitate

Thrill of victory: there's nothing to compare it to

Through any and all means possible: get the job done

Throw caution to the wind: stop worrying, worrywart, and start doing it

Throw the book at them: administering the maximum penalty allowed under the law

Throw the towel in: forfeit, you can't win

Throw you a bone: a small share

Throw your hat into the ring: becoming a participant

Throwing a line: trying to get something, fishing for it

Throwing curves: not coming directly to the point

Throwing good money after bad money: inept investing

Throwing salt on an open wound: making matters worse

Thrown to the winds: missing a great opportunity

Thrown to the wolves: mercilessly abandoned. "Abandon all hope when you enter here" (Alighieri Dante).

Thumbs up or thumbs down: up you like it, down you don't

Tickled to death: so happy

Tie one on: get drunk

Tied up in knots: too much on your mind, nerve-racked

Tighten up your belt: stop spending so much, no more superfluousness

Time heals all wounds: ashes to ashes, dust to dust

Time is a thief: it steals the past

Time is fleeting: there never seems to be enough time to do all the things you want to do

Time is money: learn and earn simultaneously

Time is running out: for all of us. "Life is like the shadow of a bird in flight" (Talmud).

Time to get away from it all: take a vacation

Time to hit the road: pack up and leave

Time to leave the nest: fend for yourself

Time to recharge your batteries: take some time off to regenerate your energy

Time to wake up and smell the roses: live each day as if it were your last. "Who can be so confident to utter this, tomorrow I will spend in bliss" (Lewis).

Tip of the iceberg: there's a great deal more involved

To be on the safe side: cover all the pitfalls

To die for: love

To each his own: by process of elimination, "the righteous of all peoples will inherit the bliss of the hereafter" (Talmud).

To hell and back: waiting in line for a long, long time

To the victor belong the spoils: spoils of war are highway robbery under the guise of patriotism. "In war imitate the actions of a tiger" (William Shakespeare).

To your heart's desire: limitless fulfillment

Together through thick and thin: cohabitating through good times and bad times

Tom, Dick, and Harry: no one in particular

Tone it down: make it less offensive

Tongue in cheek: humorous

Tongue-tied: speechless

Tons of fun: a big beautiful woman

Too big for your own britches: overly pleased with yourself

Too good to be true: finding paradise on Earth and passing away to heaven. "What if we still ride on, we two with life forever old yet new. Changed not in kind but in degree, the instant made eternity" (Robert Browning).

Too good to miss: an unforgettable moment

Too hot to handle: persona non grata, notorious

Too hot to trot: a scorcher, hotter than hell

Too little, too late: "Labor to inherit paradise, not the pit of destruction" (Talmud).

Too much of a good thing: overindulgence

Too much to ask for: permanent happiness

Too pooped to pop: exhausted

Too smart for your own good: incapable of contemplating constructive criticism

Too tall a mountain to climb: the task was simply too much for you to handle. "To cast beyond ourselves in opinion" (William Shakespeare).

Took it and ran with it: motivated by a good idea

Took them by storm: overnight popularity, instant celebrity

Took the wind out of their sails: sapped their strength, diminished their confidence

Tooth and nail: ferocious street fighting

Tooting your own horn: bragging

Tossing and turning: can't sleep, insomnia

Touch and go: it can go either way, a nail-biter

Touch base: stay in contact

Touched a nerve: so angered they lost their composure, you really pissed them off

Tough hand to play: stay or fold

Toughest pill of all to swallow: "Ay, but to die and go we know not where, to lie in cold obstruction and to rot" (William Shakespeare).

Towing the line: conforming to the status quo

Track record: your past. "Every hair on your head is counted" (New Testament).

Train of thought: cohesiveness

Treading in deep water: a dangerous situation. "Often in danger, yet still alive" (Samuel Johnson).

Treating someone like a stepchild: mistreating a person because they're not your own flesh and blood

Tree of life: population explosion

Trial and error: experimentation. "For nothing can be made sole or whole that has not been rent," (William Butler Yeats).

Tried and true: it has worked every time before

Trigger happy: prone to violence

Tripping: hallucination

Triumph of science: too many machines that ruin the Earth and kill people

Truer words were never spoken: all the great literature of the world

Trust fund baby: well-to-do nothing

Trust your instincts: sometimes it's all you have to go by

Try it on for size: see if you like it

Trying to get your goat: attempting to upset you

Trying to make a buck: money is very important

Trying to pull a fast one: scheming a scam

Trying to run before you can walk: getting ahead of yourself

Tug of war: no one wants to give an inch

Tugs at your heart strings: dramatic effect

Tune in: check it out. "Vision or imagination represents what exists eternally" (William Blake).

Turn a phase: make it succinct, clear, concise, witty

Turn back the clock: to examine the past, to prepare for the future

Turn back the hands of time: to find "thoughts that lie too deep for tears" (William Wordsworth).

Turn the page and move on: don't look back, have faith in the future

Turned the corner: coming out of a slump

Turned upside down: topsy-turvy, confusion

Turning a blind eye: pretending you did not see it

Turning in: going to bed, nighty-night

Turning over in your grave: gross misrepresentation of your work

Turning you on to it: a good thing

Turns on a dime: easy to maneuver

Turns you on: sexually stimulating, or you simply like it

Twist my arm: make me do it

Twists and turns: the path of life

Two can live as cheaply as one: total nonsense

Two can play this game: flirting

Two-faced: talking behind your back

Two for the price of one: a real bargain, the body and the spirit

Two heads are better than one: team up

Two separate worlds: the war between the sexes

Two sides to every argument: which one is right?

Two-timer: a lover who's cheating on you

Two's company, three's a crowd: "The majority is right only when it does right" (Henrik Ibsen).

Tying the knot: matrimony

Tying up the loose ends: bringing it all together, completion

Under the gun: first to act

Under the microscope: close scrutiny, a suspect

Under the stars: a sparkling umbrella

Under the weather: enduring a temporary minor illness

Unspoken agreement: words were not needed to seal the deal

Until death do we part: true love

Until hell freezes over: hold out as long as you can

Up for grabs: first come, first serve

Up front: honest

Up in arms: cause for alarm

Up the creek without a paddle: shit out of luck, beyond help

Up there: advanced in years

Up to speed: prepared to perform at your peak level

Up to your neck: overwhelmed

Upscale: lavishness

USA government: of the lawyers, by the lawyers, for the lawyers

USA medical system: an injustice. The uninsured are screwed. The insured are pawns of avaricious insurance companies that increase premiums capriciously. And the doctors are legal drug-dealing affluent cry babies who cater to the rich.

Use it or lose it: exercising the mind and body increases longevity

Use your head: think before you act

VA medical bureaucracy: riddled with incompetent charlatans who are protected by sovereign immunity. They couldn't hack it in the real world.

Variety is the spice of life: try something new, time and again

Victim of circumstances: having no control over the outcome, simply there

Victim of your own vices: excessiveness

Wade through it: sort out the mess

Waiting until the last moment: then it's too late, goodbye

Wake-up call: you were fortunate to realize, before it was too late, that you were on the wrong path. "Descend to this, and then ask no more, rich to yourself, to all beside be poor" (Bowles).

Walk a mile in my shoes: imagine what I've experienced before passing judgment

Walk lightly but carry a big stick: never be a bully but be prepared to defend yourself and the defenseless

Walk on the wild side: try something new and exciting

Walk on water: quite a feat

Walked right into it: a trap

Walking on air: happy, happy, happy. "Happy as thou art, happiness and thou must part" (Walter Landor).

Walking on cloud nine: not a care in the world

Walking on eggshells: sensitivity

Walls have ears: you never know when someone may be eavesdropping

War and peace: Peace is a greater corruptor of man than war is a destroyer of them. Man, by nature, is a territorial fighting animal. "There is no man who does not think meanly of himself for not having been a soldier" (Samuel Johnson).

War is diplomacy by another means: "Cry havoc and let loose the dogs of war"(William Shakespeare).

War is war: "The world will hold its breath when I launch Barbarossa," (Aldolph Hitler).

War with words: a true pacifist

War zone: in the thick of things

Wash your hands of it: you played no part in causing it, put it behind you

Waste of money: paying excessive taxes

Waste of time: using words during the course of self-defense

Watch your step: stay alert. "Where ruthless mortals wage incessant wars" (William Wordsworth).

Watch your tongue: don't repeat it or I'll wash your mouth out with soap

Watching what you eat: consuming food that will keep you healthy, wealthy, and wise

Water under the bridge: it's over and done with, get on with your life

Wave of the future: it's carried forward by its own momentum

Waving the flag: sunny weather patriots

Way of all flesh: you live and then you die. Don't be one of those who "buy the life of this world at the price of the world to come" (Koran).

Way off base: repugnant behavior

Way of the world: crime and punishment

We all have crosses to bear: into each life some rain must fall. "How small to others but how great to me" (Unknown).

We all knew it was coming: the breakdown of morals

We all make mistakes: I'll drink to that

We knew you when: before you became famous

Wearing thin: the same joke too many times

Weighs heavy on your mind: a sea of troubles

Weigh the pros and cons: consider all the information carefully

Weigh your words carefully: speak from the mind and heart

Well, I'll be damned: never believed it could happen

Well's running dry: nearly broke

Went by the wayside: all good things must end

Went down the drain: it was wasted

Went down the tubes: it failed

Went haywire: gone berserk

Went in one ear and out the other: not paying close attention to the speaker

Went on the blink: it's broken

Went overboard on it: doing too much of a good thing

Went postal: completely insane

Went south: a sorry deviation, it's not working like it should be

Went to bat for you: sticking up for you. "A friend in need is a friend indeed" (Unknown).

Went to the web: research on the internet

We're all children of God: and everyone is the same whether we like it or not. "Love conquers all" (Unknown).

We're like glue: sticking together, a close friendship

Wet your pants: fully frightened

Wet your whistle: have a drink

What a difference a day makes: four and twenty hours can drastically change your life

What a doozy: spectacular

What a grind: tediously tiresome

What are friends for?: to come to your aid in the time of need

What are you driving at?: get to the point

What are you looking for?: "Seek and you shall find" (New Testament).

What difference does it make?: maybe all the difference in the world

What else can you do?: stop boring me

What else is new?: I heard it a thousand times before

What goes up must come down: male orgasms, before and after

What got into you?: a sudden change of mood, bipolar

What has that got to do with the price of tea in China?: no bearing on the topic of conversation

What have you got to lose?: you may win a prize and it doesn't cost you one red cent

What is it?: whatever it be

What I wouldn't give: to know what I know now when I was much younger

What makes the world go around?: "The cause is secret but the effect is known" (Joseph Addison).

What next?: can it be worse than this

What planet are you from?: spaced out

What you don't know won't hurt you: mind your own business unless it becomes absolutely necessary to intervene

What you see is what you get: strive for integrity

Whatever: I don't care. It makes no difference to me.

Whatever happens, happens: predestination

Whatever you say: it's fine with me

What's eating you?: spit it out, tell me what's wrong

What's good for the goose is good for the gander: the law applied equally to both sexes

What's it all about?: your guess is as good as mine

What's past is past: nevertheless, your conscience and the persistence of memory force you to reflect on it

What's right is right, what's wrong is wrong: if you can tell the difference. "Nothing is good or bad but thinking makes it so" (William Shakespeare).

What's the bottom line?: cut to the chase, tell me the utmost important thing

What's the catch?: you're concealing something

What's the damage?: how much does it cost?

When in Rome, do as the Romans do: dress and act according to the situation

When it comes right down to it: life, liberty, and the pursuit of happiness are paramount

When it rains, it pours: when things are going bad, they seem to get even worse

When it's all said and done: there's nothing you can do about it

When the bell rings: the heat is on

When the chips are down: depression sets in, never say die

When the reality sets in: you'll know it, wake up

When the time is right: reap the harvest

When you least expect it: it happens and you can ill afford it

When your ship comes in: you'll strike it rich

Where do you draw the line?: between good and evil

Where it stops nobody knows: the great wheel of destiny

Where there's a will, there's a way: you can do it

Where there's smoke, there's fire: a warning signal, react

While the cat is away, the mouse will play: keep an eye on your mate, they may be playing the field

Whistle while you work: enjoying the task at hand

White collar workers: people who earn a living primarily with their minds

White knuckles: driving during hazardous road conditions

Who can you trust?: an elderly woman, a dog, and cash money

Who died and left you boss?: someone who likes to throw their weight around, a my-way-or-highway type of person

Who knows what tomorrow may bring?: make a wish

Who, what, where, and when: a mystery

Whoever got there first: original ownership of land

Who's who?: look in the book

Why don't you take a picture?: it will last longer, stop staring at me

Widen your horizons: study geography

Wild goose chase: looking for something and not finding it

Wild, wacky, and wooly: nuttier than a fruitcake but fun to be with, the life of the party

Will eat you out of house and home: a big hog with a voracious appetite

Will never let you live it down: constantly reminding you of an error in judgment

Will of iron: unstoppable

Win, lose, or draw: playing the game

Window dressing: camouflage

Window of opportunity: a chance to do something worthwhile. "Ah, make the most of what we may yet spend, before we into the dust descend" (Edward Fitzgerald).

Wine, women, and song: how a man makes time stand still

Wined and dined: a gracious host

Winging it: a spur of the moment action, ad-libbing

Wipe the slate clean: start all over again and turn over a new leaf

Wiping the floor with them: a good trouncing

Wired: speeded up, adrenalin pumping

Wisdom of the ages: recorded in books

Wise guy: a term applicable to someone in organized crime

Wish upon a star: choose any one of them, light a candle as well

Wishing and hoping: dreams do come true

Witch hunt: an out-of-control mob looking for someone to hate

With a fine-tooth comb: painstaking attention to detail

With flying colors: passing by a wide margin

With friends like you, who needs enemies?: fair weather friends who only visit when they want something. Telling you "a tale told by an idiot, full of sound and fury, signifying nothing" (William Shakespeare).

Without fanfare: no frills

Wolf's at the door: financial problems

Won't give an inch: stubborn

Won't give you the time of day: could care less about you

Won't say die: way behind but managing to stay put, keeps dodging the knockout

Won't take no for an answer: tenacious

Won't that be the day: doubt that it will ever happen, but pleased if it does

Woopsy daisy: pardon me. "To err is human" (Alexander Pope).

Words fail me: can't explain it

Work both sides of the street: kiss ass, please everybody

Work in progress: a project not yet completed

Work like a dog: use all of your senses, especially common sense

Worked like a charm: it did the trick

Working your way up the ladder: good workers get promoted

Worst-case scenario: damned to hell, a victim of Satan. "The spirit is willing but the Flesh is weak" (New Testament).

Worth their weight in gold: words from a wordsmith

Worth your salt: an asset, not a liability

Wouldn't be caught dead there: disliking an establishment immensely

Wouldn't harm a fly: a gentle, sensitive person

Wound tighter than a drum: something's eating away at you, get it off your chest and relieve the tension

Wrapped around your finger: total control over a person

Wrapping it up: putting the final finishing touches to it

Yanking your chain: she flirts but won't put out, a teaser not a pleaser. "How can I, that girl standing there, my attention fix on politics" (William Butler Yeats).

Yesterday's news: sometimes it sticks in your brain, you can't get it out of your mind

You ain't just whistling Dixie: an understatement, to say the least

You ain't seen nothing yet: I can do it even better

You and yours: yourself and your loved ones

You are what you eat: make no mistake about it

You betcha: damn right

You bet your bottom dollar: emphatically declaring you're correct

You blew it: lost when you should have won

You can dish it out but can you take it: reciprocation

You can never go home again: there's no turning back

You can run but you can't hide: somewhere along the line your past will catch up to you

You can say that again: remarkable

You can take it to the bank: count on it

You can't argue with success: unless it's accomplished by stepping on people

You can't beat them: a drink and tobacco

You can't fight city hall: sovereign immunity, eminent domain. "All government is a restraint on liberty" (Unknown).

You can't get a word in edgewise: blabbermouths won't let you put your two cents in

You can't have your cake and eat it too: the more you have, the more you want. The less you have, the more you want.

You can't judge a book by its cover: don't form an opinion until you study it

You can't please everybody: so don't even try

You can't take it with you: all the property you've acquired. "What you have inherited from your ancestors, learn it, in order to possess it" (Georg Hegel).

You can't teach an old dog new tricks: many of us are so set in our ways that beneficial change has no appeal

You can't win them all: but try to, give it your best shot

You can write your own ticket: freewill as a way of life. "As you sow, so shall you reap" (Bible).

You catch more flies with honey than with vinegar: being polite and soft-spoken will take you much further then being a sourpuss

You don't have a prayer: no chance whatsoever

You don't have jackshit: running a bluff

You don't know the half of it: knowing little, if anything, about the subject

You feel it the next morning: overdoing it

You get back what you put in: equalization

You get what's coming to you: when your time is up and your days have ended. We all have it coming.

You get what you pay for: don't be cheap, purchase quality goods

You got a problem?: a resort to a retort

You got it: I'll gladly do it for you

You got it all wrong: it was the furthest thing from my mind

You got them where you want them: in a compromising position

You go your way and I'll go mine: the end of a friendship

You have a lot of room to talk: hypocritical

You have a point: a solid opinion

You have to deal with it: whatever comes your way

You have to do what you have to do: if it must by all means be done, do it, dangerous or otherwise

You have to have a gimmick: something different that people will take notice of and like

You have to pass go to make a pass: getting a come-on for a romantic approach

You have your work cut out for you: don't we all

You hit the nail on the head: the meaning concisely said

You hold the key: to all your desires

You know it and I know it: things are just the way they are

You know the drill: you've done it many times before

You know where they're coming from: understanding perfectly what someone is like, they can't hide behind a mask

You learn something new every day: pay attention

You lost your shirt: losing a lot of money gambling. "My kingdom was but a care, I lost it, it's no longer a care" (William Shakespeare).

You made your bed so lie in it: blame no one but yourself

You mess with the bull and you get the horn: don't antagonize a strong person or nation

You never know what's going to happen: hope for the best, be prepared for the worst

You only live once: who knows? Nobody has all the answers.

You owe it to yourself: a reward for a job well done

You should know better: to do what you're doing

You suit me to a tee: two people made for each other

You take the cake: when it comes to being ridiculous, you're at the top of the list

You took the words right out of my mouth: I was just going to say the exact same thing

You will never know unless you try: maybe you can do it. The saddest words one can say are "I coulda been somebody" (Marlon Brando).

You won't get out of here alive: you know what I mean, but at least with dignity and a marked grave. "I bequeath myself to the dirt" (Walter Whitman).

You won't know until you get there: what all the trials and tribulations were for

You won't pass this way again: the time is now

You'll know better next time: live and learn

You'll never live it down: making a complete fool out of yourself

Young at heart: a youth serum

Your back's to the wall: there's nowhere to turn

Your birthday suit: stark naked, how you entered into the world

Your calling: what you were born to do

Your claim to fame: you did your best. "Sun is the gate to heaven, where only the wise can pass" (William Butler Yeats).

Your day in court: facing your accuser or the other way around

Your due and proper: a rightful share

Your eyes were bigger than your stomach: putting more food on your plate than you could eat. "Waste not, want not" (Unknown).

Your future begins today: while the past remains imbedded in your mind

Your goose is cooked: done in, finished, kaput

Your guess is as good as mine: whatever seems to be going on

Your heart's in the right place: righteousness

Your last gasp: the last thing you want to do is the last thing you do

Your last pound of flesh: pure capitalism coupled with greed

Your line of work: how you make a living

Your main squeeze: your one and only lady

Your neck of the woods: your home, where you work, and the immediate area surrounding them

Your own man: you can't be bought, you won't sell out

Your own worst enemy: self-destructiveness

Your reward will be great in heaven: if you store your treasures there. Wear your heart on your sleeve.

Your ship came in: finally success, a king's ransom

Your time will come: on judgment day before the Supreme Master of the Universe

You're asking for it: a severe reprimand, cruising for a bruising

You're barking up the wrong tree: you're not going to get what you're attempting to acquire

You're coming up in the world: better off than you were before

You're darn tootin': I agree with you 100%

You're getting on my nerves: annoying you beyond tolerance

You're not out of the woods yet: although things are improving, in regard to an unfortunate incident, be on guard until it's over

You're only human: much is out of your control

You're the limit: a wild person, too much to handle

You're the man: presently in the spotlight

You've got to give a little to get a little: loosen up

Zero in on it: find what you're looking for

Zeroing in: preparation to be right on target

Zigged when you should have zagged: you should have done it the other way

Printed in the United States
33293LVS00003B/76-204